LOST IN THE SCROLL

REDISCOVERING SANATAN IN THE DIGITAL AGE

ADITHYA KRISHNAN

ISBN
Paperback 979-8-89929-962-9
Hardcase 979-8-89984-210-8

A Special Note on this Day:

And finally, to my dear father, M.P. Krishnan, whose steadfast devotion and wisdom truly laid the path for this book: Happy Birthday, Appa! Your influence is woven into every page. My heartfelt Namaskarams.

Author's Note

As you embark on this journey through "Lost in the Scroll," I want to share a piece of my own story that profoundly shaped this book. It is fundamentally shaped by the quiet, enduring wisdom that flowed from my very first teachers: my parents, M.P. Krishnan and Rajeswari Krishnan, and my beloved grandmother, Alamelu (fondly known as Radha).

Growing up in a Brahmin household in Chennai, with our roots stretching back to Tanjavur and Palakkad, the profound pronouncements of Mahaperiyava and the intricate Advaitam of Adi Shankaracharya often felt like a gentle, sometimes insistent, hum in the background. A hum I, in my youthful rebellion, frequently tried to tune out.

Yet, life has a profound way of guiding us. During a particularly challenging period, when the foundations of my world seemed to crumble, I found myself leaning on a strength I hadn't truly understood: faith.

What felt like a miracle unfolded, bringing unexpected calm and clarity. It was then that I truly began to listen, to delve into the Bhagavad Gita and Srimad Bhagavatam, not out of duty, but out of a genuine thirst for understanding. I sought the deeper meaning behind the rituals, the culture, the very fabric of Sanatan Dharma that my parents had so steadfastly upheld.

My grandmother, Radha, whose own spiritual exploration through Brahma Kumari showed me the expansive and inclusive nature of divine connection, also served as a profound inspiration.

This book is my offering, born from that journey. It is a testament to the enduring power of those roots my family nurtured, however subtly, and to the timeless wisdom they embodied.

To my Appa, Amma, and my dear Paati, thank you. Your lives and your unwavering belief laid the foundation for every insight within these pages. This book is for you, and for every soul seeking their own steady ground in this digital age.

Glossary: Navigating the Digital Lingo

While reading the book, there are some terms you might encounter in this book that are common in today's digital landscape, especially among younger generations. Don't worry, let me break them down for you!

Add to Cart: A phrase from online shopping, meaning to select an item for purchase. Used metaphorically here to mean "choose" or "decide to engage with."

Chaotic Stir-fry: A vivid metaphor for a mix of many different things (like cultures or ideas) that can feel overwhelming or messy, rather than neatly blended.

Chill Power: A simple way to describe a strong, calm, and effortlessly cool influence or ability.

Coding Convention: A common gathering or conference for people involved in computer programming and software development.

Cosmic Fingerprint: A unique and individual mark or identity, emphasizing that each person has a distinct and essential purpose or nature.

Curated Chaos: Refers to online content (like social media feeds) that appears chaotic or overwhelming, but has actually been carefully selected and presented by algorithms or users to create a specific impression.

Cuts Through the Static: To get rid of distracting noise or irrelevant information, allowing a clear message or truth to be heard.

Digital Daze: A state of feeling confused, overwhelmed, or disoriented from too much time spent online or too much digital information.

Digital Echo Chamber: An online space where a person only encounters beliefs or opinions that match their own, reinforcing their views and isolating them from differing perspectives.

Digital Nomad: Someone who uses technology to work remotely, allowing them to travel and live in different places, often embracing a lifestyle less tied to a single physical location.

Digital Roar: The overwhelming, loud, and constant stream of information, notifications, and chatter present in the online world.

Ditching the Drama: To get rid of unnecessary conflict, stress, or emotional turmoil.

Doom-scrolling: The act of continuously scrolling through bad news or distressing content online, often leading to feelings of anxiety or despair.

Endless Buffet of Identities: A metaphor for the vast number of ways people present themselves or try on different personas online, as if choosing from a diverse offering.

Insta-Filtered World / Insta-Filter: Refers to the tendency to present a highly edited, often unrealistic, and idealized version of reality online, inspired by filters used on platforms like Instagram.

Inner Vibe: A person's true inner feeling, essence, or emotional state; a sense of personal energy or frequency.

Level Up Your Life: A term from gaming, meaning to improve one's skills, abilities, or overall situation in life, reaching a higher stage or achievement.

Mind-bending Interconnectedness: An idea of connection between things that is so profound or complex it challenges usual ways of thinking.

Pixelated (self): A metaphor for feeling fragmented, unclear, or incomplete in one's identity, like an image that isn't sharp due to low digital resolution.

Plug into something timeless: To connect with something ancient, enduring, and universally relevant, rather than just modern or fleeting trends.

Rebel with a Cause: Someone who challenges existing norms or authorities for a specific, important reason or belief.

Rebooted: To restart or refresh something, giving it a new beginning or an updated approach, like restarting a computer.

Savage Relevance: A powerful, intense, and unexpectedly sharp connection or importance to current times, often implying a raw or impactful truth.

Smashes the Isolation: To forcefully break through feelings of being alone or cut off from others, creating connection.

Steady Ground: A stable and reliable foundation or sense of security, especially in uncertain times.

TikTok Dance: A popular, often short, choreographed dance routine that goes viral on the TikTok social media platform, symbolizing fleeting online trends.

Trending Hashtag: A word or phrase preceded by a hash symbol (#) that becomes very popular on social media, indicating a widely discussed topic.

Tune In: To focus attention on something, to listen or become aware of it, like tuning a radio to a specific frequency.

Unplug from the Matrix: A reference to the movie "The Matrix," meaning to disconnect from a false or overwhelming reality (here, the digital world) to experience something more genuine or real.

Zen Master: An informal term for someone who has achieved a high level of calm, wisdom, and inner peace, often through meditative practices.

Contents

Introduction

The Buried Code

In the cosmic soap opera, we call the internet age, you're probably more clued in on the messy divorce of some reality TV star you secretly follow than, say, the epic love story of Radha and Krishna, which, let's be honest, had way more drama and infinitely better life lessons. Your brain is probably full of celebrity gossip while the actual legends of your ancestry are gathering digital dust bunnies in the forgotten corners of your mind.

We're in this relentless race to keep up with the trends of the internet, unknowingly hitting the delete button on our own identity one thumb-swipe at a time. It's like trying to download a crucial life update but accidentally overwriting your operating system with cat memes. Hilarious, sure, but not exactly functional.

Dharma is being replaced by dopamine, and viral trends are replacing wisdom. In our glorious age of endless scrolling, we're more likely to dissect the cryptic Instagram captions of some Hollywood heartthrob's breakup than, you know, the actual epic tales of our ancestors.

Remember the famous dialogue from 3 Idiots? *"Life is a race, agar tez nahi bhagoge to koi tumhe kuchal kar aage nikal jayega."* In the digital age, that race has become a frantic, multi-player online game where the prize is often just fleeting validation and the fear of being "left on seen" feels like a genuine existential crisis.

We're building shrines to social media gods and goddesses, trading the actual purpose of our existence for the fleeting dopamine rush of likes and follows. It's a tough love story with the internet – we're addicted to the connection, but it's often leaving us feeling more disconnected from ourselves and our roots than ever before.

But in this relentless, scroll-induced haze, haven't we accidentally misplaced something truly ancient? Something that wasn't just a bunch of old-timey stories, but the very DNA of our cultural identity, lying dormant beneath the layers of viral dances and meme wars?

Think about it, their wisdom shaped civilizations, their insights explored the very fabric of reality… and we're using our precious brain cells to argue about whether pineapple belongs on pizza. (Spoiler alert: it doesn't)

Here's a thought that might just make your brain do a little backflip: even those western tech gurus we practically worship, Steve Jobs, Mark Zuckerberg, Elon Musk, etc., who shaped our digital reality, felt the pull of something deeper.

They trekked to India, seeking inspiration from gurus and ashrams, looking for that ancient spark to ignite their groundbreaking ideas. And get this, even those mind-bending Hollywood blockbusters that make you question reality, like *The Matrix* with its red pill/blue pill dilemma, *Inception* with its dream layers, *Interstellar* pondering our place in the cosmos, they're all unknowingly echoing concepts that have been part of our Sanatan Dharma for ages! It's like our ancient sages were the original scriptwriters for existential sci-fi, and we're too busy watching cute cat videos to notice the connection.

There's this massive misconception floating around that Dharma is all about stuffy rituals, chanting at deities, and awkward temple visits with your extended family where your aunt keeps pinching your cheeks.

While those can be *part* of the picture for some, the real deal is that it's a whole freakin' *operating system for life*. It's the OG life hack manual, a blueprint designed to navigate the chaos of *any* era, making its relevance in our current digital dumpster fire more crucial than ever before.

What if I told you and get ready for your mind to be slightly blown, that the answers to our oh-so-modern struggles, that soul-crushing burnout from trying to be a productivity unicorn, that addictive grip of social media that makes us feel like we're missing out on a life that doesn't even exist, those relationship dramas that could be solved with a little less "seen" and a little more "self-awareness" were already being discussed around ancient campfires thousands of years ago?

Our sages weren't just chilling under trees; they were dropping wisdom bombs that could detonate our digital anxieties today.

Mind you, this book is not about preaching or creating nostalgia. I am not here to preach or wallow in nostalgia for a time when the biggest tech problem was probably a broken bullock cart. This is a rediscovery mission unearthing the timeless awesomeness that's been right under our noses (or rather, under our thumbs), dusting it off, and hacking our modern lives with ancient wisdom.

It's about reclaiming a life that feels less like a frantic scroll-a-thon and more like a balanced, purposeful journey with a seriously insightful GPS. Because let's face it, the only thing more constant than change is the nagging feeling that there's gotta be more to life than the next notification.

And guess what? There totally is.

Welcome to *Lost in the Scroll: Rediscovering Sanatan in the Digital Age* your slightly sarcastic, hopefully enlightening, and definitely not your yoga teacher's guide to finding actual meaning in this gloriously chaotic digital world.

It's rediscovering the timeless truths that truly, deeply matter. Let's get our scroll on... but with a purpose.

Chapter 1: Satya – Can You Handle It?

उद्धरेदात्मनात्मानं नात्मानमवसादयेत् ।आत्मैव ह्यात्मनो बन्धुरात्मैव रिपुरात्मनः
(Bhavat Gita: chapter 6, verse 5)

Elevate yourself through the power of your mind, and not degrade yourself, for the mind can be the friend and also the enemy of the self.

Truth in the Age of Filters

Imagine Krishna, the OG influencer, scrolling through Instagram. He sees a post:

"Follow your truth! Manifest anything! The universe is always working in your favour!"

He chuckles. If only the truth were that easy.

Today, the truth is as fragile as your Wi-Fi signal during a storm. Everyone is curating their "truth", highlight reels that conveniently skip the messy bits, exaggerated travel stories where the only "adventure" was finding a decent Wi-Fi spot, and the oh-so-popular "fake it till you make it" mantra, which often translates to "mastering the art of looking busy while scrolling TikTok."

But here's the million-dollar question your brain probably glosses over between memes: When was the last time you saw something online and believed it with zero hesitation? Exactly. It's like trusting a stranger who slides into your DMs with a "Hey gorgeous." Suspicious, right?

From deepfakes that look more real than your reflection after a late-night study session to news algorithms specifically designed to trigger maximum outrage and keep you glued to the screen, the truth has become a commodity bought, sold, and aggressively marketed. It's the ultimate clickbait. And yet, Satya, that ancient, unshakeable concept of truth, is the first and most fundamental pillar of Sanatan Dharma. It's the foundation upon which everything else is built.

Now, there's this whole misconception that Satya in Sanatan Dharma means taking a vow of silence and living like a digital hermit. While periods of blissful silence can be seriously good for your mental detox (think of it as airplane mode for your brain), Satya isn't about never speaking. It's about the *quality* of your words, not the sheer volume.

It emphasizes honest, meaningful communication – words that align with reality and are delivered with integrity. Think of it as choosing your words just like how you choose your filters: with intention and a touch of self-awareness.

So, how do we even begin to practice Satya in a world that seems to thrive on carefully crafted illusions and where "being real" is often considered a bold and slightly terrifying act?

The Cost of Truth: Lessons from the Wise

Swami Vivekananda's Uncompromising Integrity

Long before he was dropping truth bombs at global conferences and becoming a spiritual rockstar, Swami Vivekananda was just a curious kid named Narendranath.

His mom, bless her wise soul, instilled one rule early on: "Always speak the truth, no matter what the situation is."

Fast forward to exam day. Peer pressure hits, and a classmate leans over, desperate for an answer. Most of us, in that moment of panic, might have whispered something under our breath, considering it a harmless shortcut. But young Narendra? Nope. He refused. His friend was annoyed (because, duh, free answers!), the teacher remained blissfully unaware, and no one exactly threw a parade for his honesty. But that's the harsh truth about speaking the truth – it doesn't always come with immediate applause or a viral "good Samaritan" moment.

Although! There is a plot twist here: fast forward to 1893, the Chicago World Parliament of Religions. Vivekananda, standing fearlessly before a global audience, didn't start with some formal address. He just looked out and said, with genuine warmth, "Sisters and brothers of America."

That iconic moment was the raw power of his inherent truthfulness shining through. And the world? They actually listened.

Lesson? Truth isn't always the convenient option. It often requires a hefty dose of courage, the kind that says, "My integrity is worth more than a fleeting moment of approval or a slightly better grade."

The Mahabharata's Lesson on Truth: Yudhishthira's Dilemma

Even Yudhishthira – the eldest of the Pandava brothers in the Mahabharata and often revered as Dharmaputra, the embodiment of righteousness itself, found himself in a moral pickle.

Born of the deity Dharma, Yudhishthira was known throughout the ancient world for his unwavering commitment to truth and his deep understanding of ethical principles. His very name, Yudhishthira, can be interpreted as "steady in battle," but his greatest battles were often internal, fought on the grounds of morality and truth.

During the epic Kurukshetra war (for those who are unaware, think of this as ancient Game of Thrones, but with more chariots and fewer dragons), Krishna, his divine advisor, suggested a strategic "half-truth" to weaken the formidable warrior Dronacharya.

The news of his son Ashwatthama's death was the only way to make the seemingly invincible Drona lay down his arms. Bhima had indeed killed an elephant named Ashwatthama. Krishna advised Yudhishthira to announce this, but with a crucial ambiguity.

Yudhishthira, whose commitment to Satya was his superpower, hesitated. Lying? Even with a strategic purpose? That went against his entire moral code. His reputation for truthfulness was so absolute that even his enemies trusted his word. To utter something even slightly misleading was a profound internal conflict for him.

Ultimately, swayed by the urgency of the situation and Krishna's counsel that *sometimes Dharma requires a nuanced approach*, Yudhishthira uttered the words, "Ashwatthama is dead," but immediately followed it with a barely audible, इति नरो वा कुंजरो वा (whether man or elephant). Drona, distraught and believing his son was lost, laid down his weapons.

This pivotal moment raises a seriously interesting question that still echoes in our morally grey online world: Is truth always a binary – yes or no, true or false? Or does Dharma sometimes require us to navigate the messy in-between, considering context and consequences? It's like trying to decide if it's okay to use a filter that slightly exaggerates your jawline for a professional headshot. Is it "truthful" in essence, or a subtle manipulation? Yudhishthira's dilemma highlights the complex relationship between absolute truth and the practical application of Dharma in challenging situations.

Truth and Business: The Rise and Fall of Giants

In today's corporate jungle, where spin and PR stunts are practically Olympic sports, truth isn't just a nice-to-have moral accessory, it's often a crucial survival strategy.

When Lies Destroy Empires: The Fall of a Fraud

Think about that infamous billion-dollar startup that promised the moon on a stick with its "revolutionary" technology. Investors threw money at it like it was going out of style, and the media hailed its turtleneck-wearing founder as the next visionary messiah.

But behind the carefully crafted presentations and the slick marketing campaigns, it was all smoke and mirrors. The "revolutionary" tech? Non-existent. The moment the truth finally bubbled to the surface, the whole empire crumbled faster than your phone battery on low power, and the once-admired entrepreneur found themselves trading power suits for prison stripes. Ouch.

The Long Game of Honesty: Building a Legacy on Solid Ground

Now, flip the script. Consider companies that built their entire brand on integrity, transparency with their customers (even when things go wrong!), honesty in their leadership, and a genuine commitment to ethical practices.

These companies, the ones who genuinely practice Satya in their boardrooms and their marketing campaigns, gain something truly priceless: Trust. And in the long run, that hard-earned trust? It outlasts fleeting profits and viral marketing fads every single time. It's the ultimate brand loyalty that no amount of influencer marketing can truly buy.

Satya in Your Feed, Your Job, Your Life

Okay, so we're not all meditating in caves or closing billion-dollar deals (yet!). How does this whole Satya thing apply to our daily, scroll-filled, slightly chaotic lives?

Social Media: The Illusion of Perfection

Seriously, can we just collectively agree to dial back the "living my best life" posts when you're secretly scrolling through endless filtered feeds, feeling more anxious than a student before finals?

Let's try a radical experiment and be real. Share the messy bun days, the travel mishaps, the moments of genuine vulnerability. Authenticity, believe it or not, builds deeper and more meaningful connections than a perfectly posed sunset pic with three strategically placed hashtags. Which resonates more: that flawlessly edited vacation shot, or the hilarious story about getting lost and ending up at a questionable roadside diner? Exactly.

Workplace Ethics: Own Your Mess

Mess up at work? We all do it. The knee-jerk reaction might be to deflect, blame the intern, or hope it magically disappears.

But here's a pro-tip from the ancient playbook: own it. Your boss might be momentarily disappointed, but your honesty will earn you long-term respect and trust. Especially in this digital age, where every email, every Slack message, every mistake can be tracked and resurface later, honesty is not just a virtue – it's a surprisingly effective career strategy.

Relationships: Ditch the "I'm Fine" Lie

"I'm fine" is the universal relationship escape hatch (Even Ross from Friends says this). But let's be honest, true connections thrive on real emotions, on the honest sharing of your joys, your fears, and even your slightly irrational annoyances.

Suppressing your true feelings is like putting a crack in the foundation of your relationships. It might hold for a while, but eventually, it's going to crumble.

Honesty, even when it's uncomfortable, is the superglue that holds genuine bonds together.

Self-Reflection: The Ultimate Truth Check

The hardest truth you'll ever have to confront is the one you tell yourself in the quiet moments.

- Am I *actually* as disciplined as my meticulously planned-out to-do list suggests?

- Do my daily actions *truly* align with the values I loudly proclaim on social media?

- Am I maybe, just maybe, hiding my flaws behind a carefully constructed facade?

Lying to yourself is like trying to navigate with a broken compass. You might think you're heading in the right direction, but you're just getting further lost.

The moment you start sugarcoating your reality, you lose the power to change and grow. Because you can't fix what you refuse to acknowledge is broken.

Chanakya's Tweet: #SatyaRules #RealPolicy

Chanakya (c. 375 – 283 BCE), also known as Kautilya or Vishnugupta, was an ancient Indian polymath who served as an advisor and chief minister to the first Mauryan emperor Chandragupta Maurya.

He is renowned as a pioneering political thinker and strategist, and is credited with authoring the *Arthashastra*, a foundational treatise on statecraft, economic policy, and military strategy, offering pragmatic and often ruthless insights into acquiring and maintaining power.

His wisdom and political acumen played a crucial role in the establishment and expansion of the Mauryan Empire.

Even today, in a world drowning in political spin, corporate doublespeak, and carefully crafted narratives, Chanakya's ancient wisdom reminds us that truth, in the long run, is the bedrock of lasting influence. You can build a temporary castle on lies, but it'll eventually crumble. Genuine trust and respect are built on a foundation of honesty.

If Chanakya had a Twitter account back in the day, you can bet his feed would be full of gems like: "Even in the cutthroat game of thrones (or, you know, corporate ladder), truth is the ultimate long-term strategy. *#SatyaRules #RealPolicy*"

The Bottom Line: Can You Handle the Real You?

Satya isn't about winning online arguments or proving you're right in every heated debate. It's about cultivating a life lived with such unwavering honesty – with yourself and with the world – that if your entire digital footprint and your inner monologue were suddenly projected onto a giant screen for everyone to see, you'd have zero regrets.

So, the real question isn't just, can you handle the truth *out there* in the wild, unfiltered internet? It's: Can you handle the real *you*? And more importantly, are you brave enough to live & face it?

Chapter 2: Sticks and Stones May Break My Bones, But Words? Words Start Wars

अनुद्वेगकरं वाक्यं सत्यं प्रियहितं च यत् | स्वाध्यायाभ्यसनं चैव वाङ्मयं तप उच्यते
(Bhagavad Gita: Chapter 17, Verse 15)

Words that do not cause distress, are truthful, inoffensive, and beneficial, as well as regular recitation of the Vedic scriptures—these are declared as austerity of speech.

The Myth of Ahimsa

Let's be real—when you hear the word Ahimsa, what comes to mind?

Probably Gandhi, spinning a charkha, fasting for peace, and politely asking the British to leave. Or maybe a Jain monk stepping carefully to avoid stepping on a single ant. Noble, for sure.

Misunderstood Practice: Passive Inaction vs. Ahimsa

Here's the common misconception that's tripping us up: a lot of folks interpret Ahimsa as total passivity, thinking any action, even defending yourself or your loved ones, is a big no-no in the non-violence rulebook. It's like thinking the only way to win a video game is to just stand there and hope the enemies get bored. Spoiler alert: that's not going to work.

The real deal with Ahimsa? It's not about being a doormat. It's about *minimizing harm* in every situation. It's about consciously choosing the least violent option available. Sometimes, action is necessary, but it should always be guided by a deep well of compassion and a genuine desire to reduce suffering, both yours and others.

Ahimsa has been reduced to a simple idea: Don't physically harm others. But here's the truth, violence isn't just about bloodshed. You don't have to throw a punch to destroy someone. Sometimes, a tweet is enough.

Violence today comes in the form of:

- Hate comments that sting like a thousand papercuts.

- Cancel culture (publicly boycotting people or things or both) pile-ons that can obliterate someone's entire online (and sometimes real) existence.

- Character assassinations launched with the precision of a sniper's bullet (all from the comfort of your keyboard).

- Keyboard warriors who wouldn't dare utter a peep of their online vitriol to your face but will happily type out paragraphs of pure fire and fury.

Ahimsa, that profound principle of non-violence, isn't just about avoiding physical war; it's about the daily micro-interactions we have with people, online and off, in ways we often don't even register as harmful. And let's be real with ourselves for a hot second – we are spectacularly failing at it. Our digital tongues are often sharper than any sword.

So, let's talk about why Ahimsa is more relevant today than ever before.

The Twitter Mahabharata: When Hashtags Become Battlefields

Imagine if the Mahabharata happened in 2025. Instead of arrows, we'd have subtweets.

- #TeamKaurava would be all over Twitter, calling Arjuna a "privileged warrior" who had everything handed to him on a silver platter.

- #TeamPandava would be busy doxing Duryodhana, branding him a "toxic, entitled man-baby" and digging up his problematic tweets from 2012.

- Krishna? Forget divine wisdom; he'd be getting cancelled faster than you can say "gaslighting" for his "manipulative" advice to Arjuna.

- And #JusticeForKarna would be trending worldwide, fuelled by an army of misunderstood underdog stans churning out hilarious and edgy memes that somehow manage to miss the point entirely.

We laugh, but this twisted scenario is a disturbingly accurate reflection of how things often play out in our digital coliseum. One misinterpreted tweet, one bad take that goes viral, one out-of-context moment, and your entire identity can be reduced to a trending topic and a series of unflattering memes.

We are so much quicker to tear down and destroy than we are to understand, empathize, or offer grace. And that's precisely where Ahimsa steps in, not just as a "thou shalt not kill" commandment, but as a fundamental principle of "thou shalt not harm" in any way, shape, or digital form.

The Hugging Saint: Amma's Silent Revolution

Mata Amritanandamayi, affectionately known as Amma (the Hugging Saint), doesn't preach non-violence through lengthy, finger-wagging lectures. Her approach is a little more… hands-on.

She just hugs.

That's it. Over 40 million people, from world leaders grappling with global crises to ordinary villagers seeking solace, have been enveloped in one of her legendary embraces. No judgment, no lengthy sermons, just a silent offering of warmth and connection.

Now, take a moment and think about this: When was the last time you saw genuine love trending online? When did an act of simple kindness make it to the front page of your news feed, overshadowing the latest scandal or outrage?

Amma's philosophy is beautifully simple: people don't necessarily need more words; they need more love. Her entire global movement is built on the radical idea that healing and peace blossom through compassion, not conflict.

In a digital ecosystem where negativity spreads faster than a juicy rumour and outrage gets more clicks than empathy, Ahimsa isn't just about avoiding physical fights; it's about actively and consciously choosing peace, extending kindness, and fostering connection in every interaction, even the virtual ones.

The Business of Non-Violence: Patagonia's Silent Protest

Ahimsa isn't some lofty ideal reserved for ashram dwellers; it can be a powerful force in the cutthroat world of business, too. Take Patagonia, that iconic outdoor clothing brand.

Patagonia, founded by the legendary Yvon Chouinard in 1973, isn't just about selling high-quality gear that can withstand a Himalayan blizzard. They're also fiercely committed to environmental sustainability and activism, famously declaring their mission: "We're in business to save our home planet."

Here's their non-violent approach to business:

- They don't engage in aggressive attacks on their competitors.

- They don't manipulate their customers with deceptive marketing tactics.

- They actively push back against mindless consumerism and the "buy more stuff you don't need" mantra.

Instead, they laser-focus on:

- Producing sustainable and durable goods that last.

- Actively campaigning for environmental protection.

- Adhering to ethical and fair labour practices throughout their supply chain.

Remember that one Black Friday when they ran a truly revolutionary ad? It simply said: *"Don't Buy This Jacket."* They literally told people *not* to buy their product, explicitly stating that overconsumption is harmful to the planet.

And guess what happened? People didn't boycott them; they *respected* them for it. Their business actually grew because they stood for something far bigger than just turning a profit. That's modern-day Ahimsa in action – consciously choosing ethics, sustainability, and the well-being of the planet over the relentless pursuit of endless growth.

Now, let's look closer to home. Consider HCL Technologies, a global IT company.

While operating in a competitive industry, HCLTech has consistently emphasized ethical business conduct and corporate governance. Their commitment to transparency and fair dealings in their business operations reflects a form of Ahimsa by avoiding harmful or exploitative practices.

Similarly, **ITC Limited**, primarily known for its consumer goods, has made significant strides in sustainability, particularly in areas like water positivity and carbon positivity. Their efforts to create sustainable livelihoods for farmers and their focus on responsible environmental practices demonstrate a commitment to minimizing harm and contributing positively to the ecosystem and society.

These Indian companies, in their own ways, are showing that business success doesn't have to come at the expense of ethical considerations and environmental responsibility.

Where Does Our Ahimsa Go Wrong? (The Comment Section Black Hole)

Ever stumble upon a controversial reel on Instagram and immediately dive into the comment section to see the digital fireworks? You're not alone. It's like a train wreck – you know you shouldn't look, but you just can't help yourself.

Someone posting bad about Virat Kohli, Cue the fan army descending with digital pitchforks. If someone posts something good about the BJP, the opposition will Prepare for an onslaught of angry emojis and accusations.

We live in a bizarre era where comedians are facing threats (and sometimes the club they perform in is broken) simply for telling jokes. Ah, the irony of a "tolerant" online space!

If Ahimsa is so powerful, why do fail terribly at it?

1. **The Illusion of Strength in Aggression:** That fleeting feeling of power when you type out a scathing "I'll show them!" comment can be addictive. But true strength, the kind that builds bridges and fosters understanding, lies in restraint.

2. **The Reflex to React vs. the Wisdom to Respond:** Someone hurls an online insult? Our immediate instinct is to fire back with twice the venom. Ahimsa asks us to hit the pause button, take a breath (or five), and *respond* thoughtfully, rather than just *react* emotionally.

3. **The Empty Victory of Online Fights vs. the Real Impact of Compassion:** Engaging in endless comment wars might give you a temporary sense of righteousness, but spoiler alert: it rarely changes anyone's mind or makes the world a better place. True change, the kind that leaves a lasting positive impact, is fuelled by compassion and understanding

Arguing in comment sections isn't changing the world. Kindness, even in the digital realm, actually can.

Practicing Ahimsa in a Digital Age

You don't need to suddenly renounce your smartphone and become a silent internet monk. Just try incorporating these small but surprisingly powerful practices:

1. **The 5-Second (or 10-Second, Let's Be Real) Rule:** Before your fingers unleash that angry reply into the digital void, PAUSE. Count to five (or ten, if it's a particularly spicy situation). If, after that brief moment of reflection, you still genuinely believe your

comment is constructive and necessary, then go for it. But often, that pause is enough to let the emotional heat dissipate.

2. **Become a Negativity Ninja: Stop Engaging with the Toxic Waste:** Social media algorithms are like drama-loving toddlers – they reward outrage and negativity because it keeps us glued to the screen. If you consciously stop engaging with toxic content, you'll slowly start seeing less of it. Starve the beast of your attention.

3. **Sprinkle Kindness Like Confetti in Unexpected Places:** Leave a genuine compliment on someone's post (even if you don't know them). Offer helpful advice in a non-condescending way. Send a supportive message to someone who's going through a tough time online. You'd be shocked at how rare and how impactful a little digital kindness can be.

Kabir: The Poet of Peace in a World of Words

Kabir, a 15th-century mystic and poet, lived in a time of social and religious tension. Kabir (c. 1440 - c. 1518) was a highly influential mystic poet and saint of India, revered by Hindus, Muslims, and Sikhs. He was a key figure in the Bhakti movement, emphasizing a direct, personal relationship with the divine that transcended religious boundaries and rituals.

Kabir fiercely criticized what he saw as the hypocrisy and empty practices of both Hinduism and Islam, advocating for the oneness of God and the equality of all humanity.

His teachings, conveyed through simple yet profound couplets (Dohas) and songs, stressed inner experience, love, and devotion as the true path to spiritual liberation, rejecting caste distinctions and unnecessary religious formalism

His words transcended these divides, preaching a message of universal love and inner peace. He understood that the tongue, though small, could wield immense power – a power to either heal or destroy.

His verses, filled with simple yet profound wisdom, often warned against the destructive potential of harsh speech and celebrated the transformative power of kindness.

In our age of rapid-fire digital communication, where words can be weaponized with a mere tap, Kabir's wisdom reminds us that even fleeting expressions can leave lasting scars or offer profound healing. He embodied Ahimsa through his words, showing that non-violence extends to our speech, demanding mindful and compassionate communication.

Kabir's Digital Scroll

Imagine if Kabir popped up on your feed today: "Speak softly, digital warriors, for your words are the invisible threads that weave the fabric of our online world. Let them be threads of peace, understanding, and connection, not sharp-edged weapons of digital warfare."

The ultimate question, then, isn't just about winning that online argument or proving your point in the comment section. It's about what you truly want to build: a battlefield of digital animosity or a space where peace, empathy, and genuine connection can actually flourish.

They're rarely the same thing. Choose wisely, my friends. Choose wisely.

Chapter 3: Dana – Levelling Up Your Generosity

यज्ञदानतपःकर्म न त्याज्यं कार्यमेव तत् ।यज्ञो दानं तपश्चैव पावनानि मनीषिणाम् ॥
(Bhagavad Gita: Chapter 18, Verse 5)

Actions based upon sacrifice, charity, and penance should never be abandoned; they must certainly be performed. Indeed, acts of sacrifice, charity, and penance are purifying even for those who are wise.

The Digital Dumpster Fire: Are You a Data Gollum?

Time for a digital intervention, people. Grab that sleek device you can't live without.

Now, be honest.

How many screenshots are currently languishing in your camera roll, never to see the light of day again?

Memes that elicited a chuckle three months ago but now just evoke a vague sense of digital déjà vu?

Shopping carts across various online retailers, overflowing with stuff you *definitely* don't need but might *someday* want (maybe when you magically acquire a second apartment just to store it all)?

And it's not just the digital clutter, is it? We're Olympic-level hoarders in every aspect of our lives:

- **Cash:** Clutching onto it like it's the last roll of toilet paper during a pandemic, convinced that a bigger bank balance will somehow magically solve all our existential angst.

- **Knowledge:** Gatekeeping those precious career hacks or life lessons like they're state secrets, afraid that sharing might somehow diminish your shine.

- **Time:** Scrolling endlessly through the void, convincing ourselves it's "self-care" while our to-do list glares at us from the corner of our screen.

- **Attention:** Chasing the fleeting validation of likes and followers, trading genuine, meaningful connections for the superficial applause of the digital masses.

- **Followers:** Obsessed with vanity metrics, accumulating digital nodding heads that rarely translate into actual support or connection. Somewhere along the way, we started believing that success = accumulation.

Somewhere along our modern journey, we bought into the lie that success equals accumulation – the more you have, the more you are. But Sanatan Dharma flips that script faster than a viral TikTok dance. It whispers a counter-intuitive truth: true abundance, the kind that nourishes your soul and enriches your life, flows from giving, not grasping.

Enter Dana! The ancient art of generosity. The problem? In a world where everything, including "authenticity," is monetized, genuine, selfless giving feels as rare as a decent public restroom. We're conditioned to ask, "What's in it for me?" before we even consider opening our digital or actual wallets.

But here's a secret, a genuine life hack passed down through millennia: giving isn't just a virtuous act of kindness; it's the smartest investment you can ever make. Let's break down this ancient wisdom for our modern minds.

Guru Wisdom: The King Who Gave It All Away

One of the most legendary tales of Dana, a story that sticks with you like a particularly catchy (and slightly annoying) jingle, comes from the life of King Rantideva.

King Rantideva wasn't your average power-hungry monarch hoarding gold and territory. Nope, this dude was renowned throughout the land for his exceptional generosity and profound selflessness. He was celebrated for his unwavering compassion, a guy who felt the suffering of others in his very bones.

His devotion to Vishnu wasn't just about rituals; it was about embodying the divine qualities of empathy and giving, ultimately leading him to liberation. Talk about a glow-up!

One fateful day, after enduring days of intense fasting (we're talking serious hunger pangs here), Rantideva finally received a meagre portion of food and a sip of water. Relief was in sight! But just as he was about to take that first, glorious bite:

- A hungry beggar arrived at his doorstep, weak with starvation. Without a second thought, Rantideva gave away half of his precious meal.

- Then, a traveller stumbled in, parched and desperate for water. Rantideva didn't hesitate; he offered his only sip.

- Finally, a sick man, shivering and weak, appeared seeking nourishment. Rantideva, with a heart overflowing with compassion, gave away the remaining morsel of his food.

By the end of this rapid-fire generosity gauntlet, King Rantideva had absolutely nothing left for himself. He had endured days of hunger, and now, when relief was within reach, he had given it all away.

When asked by his attendants why he would subject himself to such extreme hardship, his reply was simple, profound, and utterly devoid of self-pity:

"I do not desire a kingdom, nor heaven, nor even liberation itself. My only desire is that no living being should ever suffer from hunger and thirst."

This, my friends, is the raw, unfiltered essence of Sattvic Dana, giving not out of obligation, not for recognition, and certainly not expecting a cosmic Venmo payment in return. It's giving because the suffering of others moves you. After all, you recognize the interconnectedness of all beings.

And here's the mind-bending part: this kind of selfless giving, strangely enough, always seems to boomerang back in unexpected ways. Maybe not as a direct reward, but as a profound sense of inner peace, stronger relationships, or a deeper connection to something larger than yourself.

Modern economists might try to intellectualize this with fancy terms like "the abundance mindset" and the "law of reciprocity." Sanatan Dharma? It just calls it Dharma – the natural order of things when you align yourself with compassion and generosity.

Generosity in the Corner Office: The Quiet Impact of Azim Premji

You might not immediately associate the cutthroat world of billionaires with the gentle principle of Dana. But then you meet Azim Premji, the former chairman of Wipro, a man who steered a small cooking fat company into a global IT powerhouse over four decades. They even call him the "Czar of the Indian IT Industry," which sounds pretty powerful, right?

Well, this incredibly wealthy and influential man did something that sent ripples of surprise through the often-self-congratulatory corporate world: he gave away over 50% of his personal wealth. Not just a casual donation here and there, but a massive, irrevocable commitment to philanthropy.

And here's the mic drop moment:

- He never craved the spotlight for his generosity.

- You won't find his name plastered on every school his foundation built.

- His focus was solely on ensuring his wealth worked for the betterment of others, not just padding his already substantial bank balance.

Most people in that stratosphere build impenetrable walls around their fortunes, creating legacies of personal wealth. Azim Premji? He built bridges, connecting his resources to the needs of education and rural development across India.

And that, my friends, is precisely why his impact on the world will far outlive any number on a Forbes list. His Dana wasn't about ego; it was about genuine contribution.

The Dana Spectrum: From "Look at Me!" to Pure Heart

Sanatan Dharma, in its wisdom, breaks down the act of giving into three distinct flavors:

1. **Tamasic Dana (The "Look at My Halo" Giveaway):** Giving motivated by guilt, obligation, or purely for show. Think posting those donation receipts on social media with a self-congratulatory caption, fishing for likes and validation. ("Just donated! #Blessed #MakingADifference #LookAtMe") Yep, that's often this category.

2. **Rajasic Dana (The "Quid Pro Quo" Kind of Kindness):** Giving with clear expectations of a return favor, recognition, or some kind of transactional benefit. ("I'll donate to your campaign, but make sure my name is prominently displayed on the building.") It's less about pure generosity and more about a strategic exchange.

3. **Sattvic Dana (The "Silent Giver" Vibe):** Giving freely, wholeheartedly, without any expectation of reward or recognition. Think about anonymously helping a stranger, sharing your hard-earned knowledge without wanting anything back, or simply offering a hand because it's the right thing to do. This is the gold standard of generosity.

The irony? The folks who give purely, without any strings attached, often end up receiving the most profound and unexpected returns: inner peace, genuine connection, and a deep sense of purpose. The universe has a funny way of balancing things out.

Why Are We So Bad at This Whole Generosity Thing?
(Let's Face the Mirror)

Let's have another real talk moment. When it comes to genuine, selfless giving, many of us are... well, let's just say there's room for improvement. Here are some common mental roadblocks:

1. **The "I'll Give When I'm Rich" Delusion:**

   Reality check: Generosity isn't a switch that magically flips when your bank account hits a certain number. If you're not inclined to share when you have ₹100, you won't suddenly transform into a philanthropic superhero when you have ₹10 lakh.

Giving is a habit, a muscle you need to exercise, not a budget decision you make once you hit a certain income bracket.

2. **The "What's the ROI on Kindness?" Mindset:**

If you're constantly keeping score every time you lend a hand or offer support, that's not generosity; that's networking with extra steps. True giving flows freely, without the expectation of a direct return on investment. It's about the outflow, not the potential inflow.

3. **The "I Don't Have Enough to Give" Lie:**

Newsflash: Generosity isn't solely about money. You have a wealth of other things to offer – your time, your skills, your knowledge, your genuine attention, a listening ear, a word of encouragement. You have far more in your arsenal than you probably realize.

Dana Hacks for the Digitally Distracted

Good news! Giving in the digital age is easier than ever. Here are some modern twists on ancient wisdom:

- **Share Knowledge Like It's Going Out of Style:** Don't hoard those valuable career hacks, those life lessons you've learned the hard way. Share your secrets, help someone else grow, and watch the collective knowledge rise.

- **Time is the Ultimate Flex: Use It Generously:** Call a friend who's struggling instead of just liking their sad post. Offer to mentor someone online for free. Simply lend a listening ear without judgment. Your time and attention are incredibly valuable.

- **Be a Generosity Influencer (The Good Kind):** Offer genuine compliments online. Share someone else's work without expecting a shoutout in return. Promote others' talents and achievements. Be a rising tide that lifts all boats.

- **Donate Smarter, Not Just Bigger:** Support small creators whose work resonates with you. Contribute to local charities making a tangible difference. Even a small amount directed to the right place can have a significant impact.

- **Digital Declutter with a Purpose:** Got a digital graveyard of 500+ saved articles you swear you'll "read later"? Be honest, you probably won't. Share the best ones with friends or online communities instead. Your digital trash could be someone else's treasure trove of knowledge.

Aryabhata's Digital Drop: #ShareTheCosmicKnowledge

Aryabhata, a 5th-century Indian mathematician and astronomer, was a true OG in the realm of knowledge sharing.

In a time when information was scarce and often guarded by select groups, he openly and freely shared his groundbreaking discoveries about the Earth's rotation, the solar system, and the revolutionary concept of zero. This wasn't just about intellectual curiosity; it was a fundamental act of generosity towards humanity's collective understanding of the universe.

Aryabhata's life and work embody the very spirit of Sattvic Dana, giving without any expectation of personal gain, driven by a deep understanding that true wealth lies in the collective advancement of knowledge. He wasn't looking for fame or fortune; he was driven by the profound desire to illuminate the mysteries of the cosmos for all.

In our digital age, where information is abundant yet often siloed, monetized, or deliberately obscured, Aryabhata's example shines as a beacon. It reminds us that true generosity in the realm of knowledge is about liberating it, making it accessible, and fostering a culture of shared learning, not locking it away behind paywalls or intellectual gatekeeping.

Imagine if Aryabhata dropped a digital scroll today: *"Knowledge, like the universe itself, expands exponentially when it's shared freely. Don't hoard your insights; drop the knowledge, and watch it illuminate the minds of many."*

So, the ultimate question boils down to this: are you going to hoard your resources, both tangible and intangible, like a digital-age miser, or are you going to choose to flow with generosity like a life-giving river? One leads to stagnation and isolation; the other to growth, connection, and a world that's just a little bit brighter. The choice, as always, is yours.

Chapter 4: Dharma vs. Drama – Finding Purpose in Chaos

कर्मण्येवाधिकारस्ते मा फलेषु कदाचन ।मा कर्मफलहेतुर्भूर्मा ते सङ्गोऽस्त्वकर्मणि || 47 || *(Bhagavad Gita: Chapter 2, Verse 47)*

You have a right to perform your prescribed duties, but you are not entitled to the fruits of your actions. Never consider yourself to be the cause of the results of your activities, nor be attached to inaction.

Lost in the Algorithm: The Modern Priority Meltdown

Picture this: It's 7 AM, and your eyes are barely open, but here you are, doomscrolling on your phone. Reels blazing on your phone, eager to read WhatsApp notifications, and unruly expectations from HR who have ghosted you.

Your eyes, still blurry with sleep, are instantly assaulted by the digital deluge:

- Your WhatsApp family group chats erupt in a predictable political squabble, each side armed with their arsenal of forwarded "facts" and fiery emojis.

- Instagram influencers, their faces perpetually bathed in golden hour lighting, urging you to "rise and grind" while casually sipping $12 lattes, conveniently ignoring the privilege that oils their hustle.

- LinkedIn posts from self-proclaimed "gurus" subtly (or not so subtly) guilt-tripping you into adopting their extreme morning routines, suggesting that anything short of waking up at 4 AM for a cold plunge and a green smoothie is a recipe for utter failure.

By 7:05 AM, a mere five minutes into your day, your brain already feels like it's run a digital marathon. You're bombarded with opinions, expectations, and manufactured urgency, leaving you feeling drained and directionless before you've even had a cup of coffee.

Welcome to modern chaos, a relentless barrage of notifications, emails, and viral trends. Everything screams for your precious focus, yet very little truly nourishes your soul or aligns with what deeply matters.

Sanatan Dharma teaches that life isn't about reacting to noise. It's about aligning yourself with Dharma—your higher purpose. Although how do we separate Dharma from Drama in an age where everything competes for our attention?

In an age where every fleeting trend and every outrage-fuelled headline vies for our attention, how do we possibly discern our Dharma from the relentless Drama? How do we cut through the noise and identify that still, small voice of purpose within? Let's seek guidance from those who, even amidst their chaotic circumstances, managed to master this crucial distinction.

The Prince Who Walked Away: The Story of Arjuna's Existential Crisis

If you think navigating your overflowing inbox and your complicated family dynamics is chaotic, try stepping into the sandals of Arjuna on the battlefield of Kurukshetra. Talk about a pressure cooker of epic proportions!

His situation wasn't just a bad day at the office; it was pure, unadulterated drama on a cosmic scale:

- **Family loyalty versus his sacred warrior duty:** He stood facing his own relatives, teachers, and respected elders, poised to engage in a war that would pit family against family. The emotional weight of this conflict was crushing.

- **Raw, conflicting emotions versus his responsibility as a warrior:** Grief, confusion, and a profound sense of moral ambiguity washed over him, threatening to drown his sense of duty and righteousness.

- **Crippling self-doubt versus his perceived destiny:** Was this senseless bloodshed truly his Dharma, his ordained path? Or was he merely a pawn in a larger, tragic game?

With the battle lines drawn and the conch shells blaring, signalling the imminent start of the war, Arjuna completely froze. In a moment of profound existential despair, he dropped his mighty bow, Gandiva, and declared, with a resounding "Nah, I'm good," his refusal to fight. He was utterly lost, unable to distinguish between the overwhelming drama of the situation and his true Dharma.

That's when his charioteer, friend, and divine guide, Krishna, stepped in with the ultimate clarity check, a timeless wisdom bomb for the ages: "Your duty is bigger than your fleeting doubts. Your Dharma, the very essence of who you are and what you are meant to do, is far more significant than your current emotional turmoil. Level up, Arjuna, and act accordingly."

The moment Arjuna stopped wallowing in the dramatic complexities of the situation and began to understand his higher purpose, his role as a warrior upholding righteousness, he was able to refocus and ultimately fulfil his Dharma.

Now, take a good, hard look at your own life. What's *your* battlefield?

- The career choice you keep agonizing over and postponing due to the fear of making the "wrong" decision?

- The paralyzing fear of failure that's holding you hostage in your comfort zone, preventing you from taking meaningful action towards your goals?

- A toxic friendship or relationship that constantly drains your energy and pulls you away from your well-being and aspirations?

Drama isn't just the juicy gossip you overhear or the explosive arguments you witness. It's anything any person, any situation, any internal resistance, that consistently pulls you away from your Dharma, from the things that truly align with your values and your sense of purpose.

Dharma in the Boardroom: Kiran Mazumdar-Shaw's Unwavering Purpose

Kiran Mazumdar-Shaw, a true visionary, single-handedly revolutionized India's biotechnology industry. But her journey wasn't a smooth, upward trajectory. In fact, when she first started, the world seemed determined to not take her seriously.

Back in the late 1970s, biotechnology was a frontier field, and certainly not one where women in India were expected to lead, let alone succeed. Banks flat-out refused to fund her ambitious ventures.

Industry experts, with their condescending pronouncements, told her that biotech had absolutely no future in India. Potential investors turned her away, one after another. She faced a mountain of scepticism and could have easily succumbed to the drama of doubt and discouragement.

But Kiran Mazumdar-Shaw understood a fundamental truth: Dharma isn't about chasing fleeting trends or taking the path of least resistance. It's about staying fiercely true to your inner calling, to your deeply held purpose, even when the entire world seems to be telling you to quit.

Instead of chasing short-term profits or jumping ship to a more "promising" industry for quick success, she remained steadfastly committed to her vision: making life-saving medicines affordable and accessible to the people who needed them most.

Today, Biocon, the company she founded, stands as one of India's largest and most respected biopharmaceutical companies, providing low-cost insulin to millions and firmly placing India on the global biotech map.

Dharma isn't about chasing trends or taking the easy road —it's about staying true to your purpose.

Her lesson?

Drama is often the seductive allure of chasing money, fleeting fame, or trendy pursuits that don't resonate with your core values. Dharma, on the other hand, is the quiet, persistent work of building something truly meaningful, something that contributes to the greater good, even when you're the only one who believes in its potential.

Why Are We Such Drama Magnets?

So, if aligning with our Dharma is so crucial for a fulfilling life, why do so many of us find ourselves perpetually entangled in the sticky web of drama? Here are a few key reasons why we often prioritize the superficial noise over the profound purpose:

1. **The Tyranny of Urgency Over the Quiet Power of Importance:** Our modern world is designed to bombard us with a constant sense of urgency.

   Emails demanding immediate responses, social media notifications flashing like emergency signals, "URGENT!!!" texts that often turn out to be anything but. Just because something is loud and insistent doesn't automatically equate to its importance in the grand scheme of your Dharma.

2. **The All-Consuming Black Hole of FOMO (Fear Of Missing Out):** The curated perfection of social media feeds constantly whispers the insidious lie that everyone else is living a more exciting, more fulfilling life than you are.

   This fuels a relentless chase of trends, viral content, and even the dreams of others, pulling us further away from identifying and pursuing our own unique Dharma. Dharma requires focused intention; drama thrives on scattered distraction.

3. **The Uncomfortable Truth: Our Unconscious Addiction to Conflict:** We often *say* we crave peace and tranquility, but let's be brutally honest with ourselves: how many of us secretly enjoy the adrenaline rush of gossip, the self-righteousness of online arguments, the vicarious thrill of outrage?

   Drama can provide a temporary, albeit toxic, form of stimulation.

4. **The Siren Song of Instant Gratification:** Drama often provides immediate, albeit shallow, dopamine hits, the rush of a heated

argument, the validation of a viral tweet, the temporary distraction from our own deeper issues.

Dharma, on the other hand, is often a marathon, requiring sustained effort and delayed gratification, which can feel less immediately rewarding.

How to Navigate the Drama Minefield and Actually Follow Your Dharma

Want to cut through the incessant noise and finally focus on what truly matters in your life? Try incorporating these practical strategies:

1. **The "Will This Matter in 5 Years?" Rule:** Before you react to a problem, get sucked into an argument, or spend hours obsessing over a minor inconvenience, ask yourself this simple yet powerful question: "Will I even remember or care about this in five years?"

   If the answer is a resounding "no," then consciously choose to let it go and redirect your energy towards something more aligned with your long-term purpose.

2. **The "3 Priorities Only" Rule:** Every morning (or the night before), take a few moments to identify the three most important things that truly align with your Dharma for that day. These should be the tasks, actions, or intentions that will move you closer to your higher purpose.

   Then, consciously commit to focus on these three priorities and, as much as possible, ignore everything else that clamours for your attention.

3. **Unsubscribe from the Unnecessary and Unfollow the Frivolous:** Your mental real estate is precious. Don't rent it out to negativity and distractions. Unfollow accounts that consistently peddle drama or make you feel inadequate. Exit those toxic WhatsApp groups that thrive on gossip and outrage.

   Mute notifications from apps that constantly interrupt your focus. Curate your digital environment like you curate your physical space – keep only what nourishes and supports you.

4. **Return to Your "Why": The Compass of Your Dharma:**
   Whenever you feel lost, overwhelmed by drama, or unsure of your
   direction, take a moment for introspection. Ask yourself: "What is
   my Dharma? What am I here to do? What are my core values, and
   how can I align my actions with them?"

   Regularly returning to your "why" will help you recalibrate your
   internal compass and navigate the chaotic seas of modern life with
   greater clarity and purpose.

Adi Shankaracharya: The Original Mindset Master Who Saw Through the Illusion

Adi Shankaracharya, the brilliant 8th-century philosopher and sage,
was a master of discerning the ultimate truth from the illusions of the
world. He understood that the external world throws an endless barrage
of distractions our way, but true progress, true fulfilment, comes from
cultivating inner stillness and achieving clarity of purpose.

His profound teachings, which synthesized various schools of thought,
emphasized the importance of self-realization, understanding your true
nature beyond the fleeting dramas of the ego and the material world.

In our hyper-stimulated world, where our attention is constantly
being pulled in a million different directions, Adi Shankaracharya's
wisdom serves as a timeless reminder that true power lies not in endlessly
reacting to every external force but in anchoring ourselves to our inner
Dharma, our intrinsic truth.

Imagine Adi Shankaracharya dropping a metaphorical mic at a TED
Talk: *"The biggest illusion you face is confusing constant movement with
actual progress. Find stillness within the chaos. Know your Dharma, your
essential purpose. Everything else, the endless noise and drama, is ultimately
just background noise."*

So, the most crucial question you can ask yourself, in any given
moment, is this: Is what I'm focusing on right now truly aligned with
my Dharma, with my higher purpose? Or is it just another fleeting
distraction, another act in the never-ending play of drama?

Your answer holds the key to finding purpose in the chaos.

Chapter 5: Kshama – The Power of Letting Go

क्रोधाद्भवति सम्मोह: सम्मोहात्स्मृतिविभ्रम: |स्मृतिभ्रंशाद् बुद्धिनाशो बुद्धिनाशात्प्रणश्यति || 63 || (Bhagavad Gita: Chapter 2, Verse 63)

Anger leads to clouding of judgment, which results in bewilderment of memory. When memory is bewildered, the intellect gets destroyed; and when the intellect is destroyed, one is ruined.

The Secret Addiction: Why We Hoard Grudges Like Limited-Edition Sneakers

Let's have a brutally honest heart-to-heart, shall we? We, as a species, have a sneaky little addiction to holding onto grudges. Deny it all you want, but deep down, you know it's true.

✓ Your ex ghosted you after you shelled out for that ridiculously overpriced, Instagram-worthy dinner? Grudge unlocked; achievement earned.

✓ Your roommate, in a moment of pure culinary anarchy, devoured your last, sacred slice of pizza? Grudge activated, internal fury simmering.

✓ Your so-called "friend" dared to roast your unwavering (and consistently disappointing) support for Royal Challengers Bangalore after yet another soul-crushing defeat? Grudge loading… prepare for passive-aggressive memes.

We even wear our grudges like some twisted badge of honour, a testament to the injustices we have endured. "Oh, you know what *he* did? I will *never* forget that!" Sound like a familiar soundtrack to your internal monologue?

Well, here's the unvarnished truth, served piping hot: holding onto anger is like you're willingly paying rent for prime real estate in your head to someone who, statistically speaking, is probably living their best life and hasn't given your existence a second thought since the perceived offense.

Sound familiar? You're the one stuck with the leaky emotional roof and the noisy neighbours of resentment.

And here's the kicker: while you're busy meticulously curating your mental grudge museum, you're the one carrying the actual weight. That bitterness isn't a burden on them; it's a hefty backpack full of negativity strapped squarely to *your* shoulders.

Sanatan Dharma's ancient wisdom on Kshama, often translated as forgiveness, isn't some fluffy, New Age concept about being a spineless doormat. It's about being incredibly mentally and emotionally savvy, a strategic move for your own well-being.

Forgiveness isn't about letting others off the hook for their actions; it's about liberating yourself from the corrosive burden of negativity that eats away at your peace like digital termites in your mental hard drive.

And if this ancient wisdom feels a bit like dusty scrolls in a digital world, let's talk about a warrior from those very epics who understood the profound power of letting go better than your most insightful therapist.

The Warrior Who Chose Peace Over Vendetta: The Inspiring Story of Karna

If anyone in the Mahabharata had a legitimate laundry list of reasons to hold onto a monumental grudge, it was Karna. This guy was dealt a truly unfair hand from the very beginning:

- Abandoned at birth by his own mother, left to the whims of fate? Check.

- Publicly humiliated and constantly denigrated for his supposed low birth, despite his extraordinary abilities? Double-check, with extra emphasis on the sting of social exclusion.

- Denied his rightful place as the eldest of the Pandavas and the heir to the throne, all because of societal prejudice? Triple-check, with a side of existential angst.

Yet, when the ultimate truth was finally revealed – that he was indeed the eldest of the Pandava brothers and the rightful heir to the throne he had been denied – Karna faced a pivotal choice: unleash a full-blown villain mode on the brothers who had unknowingly scorned him, fuelled by years of resentment, or choose a different, more profound path.

In a move that speaks volumes about the power of Kshama, Karna, despite the deep wounds inflicted upon him, ultimately chose forbearance. He might have harboured a justified side-eye for his mother, Kunti, for her initial abandonment, but he ultimately didn't allow bitterness and the burning desire for revenge to completely define his actions. He faced the world's inherent unfairness with a stoic "it is what it is" attitude and remained steadfast to the Dharma he had chosen.

The enduring lesson from Karna's complex life?

Karma, the cosmic law of cause and effect, will ultimately handle justice in its own way and its own time. Your primary job is to not allow the toxic poison of resentment to fester within you, warping your personality and stealing your inner peace.

Now, take a moment of honest self-reflection. What grudge are you currently holding onto that's silently weighing you down, dimming your light?

- A colleague who betrayed your trust in a professional setting?

- That person on a dating app who ghosted you after weeks of promising chats?

- A past mistake, a personal failing, that you just can't seem to forgive yourself for?

Karna's powerful story serves as a potent reminder that choosing to let go of resentment isn't hitting the "weak" button; it's hitting the "power" button, reclaiming your emotional sovereignty.

Forgiveness in Business: Anand Mahindra's Resilience After the Scorpio "Oof" Moment

Fast forward from ancient epics to the late 1990s, a time when the internet was still finding its footing and Indian businesses were stepping onto the global stage.

Anand Mahindra's company, Mahindra & Mahindra, experienced a major "oof" moment that could have easily spiralled into a blame game of epic proportions.

In a bold move to compete in the global SUV market, Mahindra & Mahindra launched the Scorpio. But the initial models? Let's just say they weren't exactly winning any design or engineering awards. They faced a series of engineering fails, marketing flops that left consumers scratching their heads, and ambitious expansion attempts that face-planted harder than a toddler learning to walk.

In such a high-stakes situation, the natural human tendency would be to start pointing fingers faster than a TikTok dance trend. Who was to blame? Should they fire the entire engineering team? Sue the hapless marketing agency? Hold a collective grudge against the entire fiercely competitive automotive industry?

But Anand Mahindra chose a different, more enlightened path: Kshama. He consciously forgave the mistakes, the costly setbacks, the collective facepalms that must have echoed through the boardroom. Instead of dwelling in the quagmire of the past and assigning blame, he focused on the crucial "glow-up."

He rebuilt his team with renewed vision, levelled up the product with crucial improvements, and, through perseverance and a forward-thinking mindset, turned the Mahindra Scorpio into a massive global SUV success.

Today, the Scorpio (*though I personally prefer XUV 700*) stands as a testament to resilience and the power of moving forward. Its success wasn't born out of revenge or dwelling on past failures, but out of the conscious decision to forgive, learn, and rebuild.

The business lesson, and the life lesson, is clear: Grudges are like dial-up internet for your personal and professional growth, slow, frustrating, and ultimately hindering your progress.

Forgiveness, on the other hand, is the fibre optic connection that allows you to process, learn, and move forward at lightning speed.

Why Forgiving Feels Like Doing the Dishes (Something We Masterfully Avoid)

Let's be brutally honest again: forgiving someone who has hurt you, or even forgiving yourself for past mistakes, often feels about as appealing as tackling a mountain of dirty dishes after a massive feast. We know we *should* do it, but we'll find a million other things to procrastinate on first.

Here's why this essential act of emotional hygiene feels so damn difficult:

1. **We Confuse Forgiveness with Being a Pushover:**

   The ego whispers insidious lies like, "If I forgive them, they'll think I'm weak, a total softie they can walk all over."

   But the reality is, forgiveness isn't about saying "it's cool" when it's absolutely not. It's about refusing to let their BS take up permanent residence in your precious brain space, rent-free. True strength lies in your ability to choose your own emotional landscape.

2. **We Crave Revenge More Than Resolution (Admit It):**

   That primal urge for justice, for the other person to suffer as much as you did, can be incredibly powerful. "They hurt me deeply. They *should* suffer the consequences!"

   But the cold, hard truth is, they're probably living their lives, blissfully unaware of the emotional turmoil you're still wrestling with, and haven't thought about the incident since. Meanwhile, you're the one mainlining the pain and keeping the wound fresh.

3. **We Mistakenly Believe Forgiveness Equals Reconciliation (Awkward Birthday Parties, Anyone?):**

The thought of forgiving someone often conjures up images of forced apologies and uncomfortable reunions. "If I forgive them, does that mean I have to invite them to my birthday party and pretend everything's okay?" Absolutely not!

You can wholeheartedly forgive someone for your own inner peace and still hit "block" on all their social media accounts and strategically avoid them at family gatherings. Boundaries are your best friend in the forgiveness journey.

Kshama Hacks: Unsubscribing from the Toxic Newsletter of Bitterness

Ready to finally stop carrying around that heavy emotional baggage? Try these practical life hacks to unsubscribe from the toxic newsletter of bitterness:

- **The "Letter You'll Never Send" Exercise: Unleash the Unspoken:**

  Take out a pen and paper (or open a new document). Write a raw, unfiltered letter to the person who hurt you. Pour out every single feeling – your anger, your sadness, your disappointment, your frustration. Say everything you've ever wanted to say, without holding back.

  Then, once you've emptied your emotional reservoir onto the page, take that letter and burn it (safely, of course) or delete the file. This symbolic act can provide a powerful sense of release without the messy confrontations or the need for the other person to even know.

- **Stop Replaying the Scene: Change the Channel on Your Mental TV:**

  The more you mentally replay the betrayal, the insult, or the injustice, the deeper it gets etched into your psyche. It's like watching the same sad movie on repeat – it just reinforces the negative emotions.

Consciously make an effort to interrupt this cycle of rumination. The moment you catch yourself replaying the scene, actively hit "pause" on your mental TV and deliberately replace it with a happy memory, a goal you're currently crushing, or a calming visualization.

- **Mirror Check: You're Not Exactly a Saint Either (Embrace Imperfection):**

Take a moment for honest self-reflection. Remember that time you accidentally (or maybe not so accidentally) stepped on someone else's metaphorical toes? Perhaps you said something you regretted, acted selfishly, or made a mistake that hurt someone else.

Wouldn't you, in those moments, want a little Kshama, a little understanding and forgiveness, in return? Cultivating empathy for others' imperfections can make it easier to extend that same grace to those who have wronged you.

- **Boundaries > Walls: Forgive Wisely, Protect Fiercely:**

Forgiving someone doesn't mean opening the floodgates and inviting repeat offenders back into your life without any safeguards. You can wholeheartedly forgive someone for your own inner peace and still build strong, healthy boundaries to protect yourself from future harm.

Forgive, learn from the experience, and then build Fort Knox around your emotional well-being, carefully choosing who gets access.

Final Thought: If Emperor Ashoka Had a Livestream… #PeaceOutGrudges

Emperor Ashoka, who ruled a vast empire in ancient India during the 3rd century BCE, was initially known for his fierce military conquests. However, after the brutal Kalinga War, witnessing the immense suffering and devastation he had caused, he underwent a profound transformation.

Deeply remorseful for the bloodshed, he embraced Buddhism and dedicated the rest of his reign to promoting peace and Dharma (righteous conduct).

Despite wielding immense power and having the ability to exact swift revenge on those who opposed him, Ashoka consciously chose the path of non-violence and forgiveness. He issued edicts inscribed on pillars and rocks throughout his empire, promoting compassion, understanding, and the welfare of all beings.

His radical transformation stands as a powerful historical example of choosing Kshama over aggression, even on a massive, empire-altering scale.

Imagine if Emperor Ashoka had a livestream today, broadcasting his wisdom across the digital realm: *"The greatest victory is not the conquest of lands, but the conquering of your own inner anger and resentment. Choose peace over conflict. Choose Kshama over bitterness. Let #DharmaOverDrama be your guiding principle."*

So, the ultimate question for you, dear reader, is this: are you going to allow the heavy, discordant notes of grudges to be the background music of your life, constantly playing on repeat and draining your energy? Or are you finally ready to drop that beat, release the negativity, and move on to a more harmonious and peaceful existence?

The remote control to your inner peace is in your hands. Choose wisely.

Chapter 6: Satyam – Level Up Your Honesty (No Cap)

सत्यं ब्रूयात् प्रियं ब्रूयात्, न ब्रूयात् सत्यम् अप्रियम् । प्रियं च नानृतम् ब्रूयात्, एष धर्मः सनातन: ॥ *(Bhagavad Gita: Chapter 10, Verse 4-5)*

Speak the truth which is pleasing to others, do not speak the truth which is displeasing; do not speak untruth which is pleasing either; this is the eternal dharma.

The Art of the Half-Truth: Why Our Honesty-O-Meter is Constantly Glitching

Well, to be honest, lying, in its various shades and forms, often feels like the path of least resistance. It's the mental shortcut we take when the truth feels too complicated, too awkward, or it potentially might have some consequences.

- Running late for that brunch you swore you'd be on time for? "Traffic was absolutely savage!" *(The snooze button got a solid three rounds.)*

- Trying to gracefully bow out of that cringe-inducing party your distant cousin is throwing? "Oh man, feeling a bit under the weather today." *(Actual diagnosis: a deep dive into Netflix and the comforting embrace of your couch.)*

- Dangerously behind on that crucial work deadline your boss is hounding you about? "Almost there! Just putting the final touches on it." *(Reality: you're still staring at a blinking cursor on a blank document, with coffee and existential crisis.)*

These little white lies, these convenient omissions, these carefully crafted half-truths – they start small, like digital dust bunnies under the rug of our conscience. They have a sneaky way of multiplying, of breeding more elaborate deceptions until, before you know it, you're living in your own personal reality show of carefully curated falsehoods.

You're not just bending the truth for others; you're starting to believe your own spin.

Sanatan Dharma, with its timeless wisdom, places Satyam (truthfulness) on a pedestal, recognizing it as a foundational pillar of a righteous life. But it's not just about avoiding those full-blown, pants-on-fire whoppers that would make Pinocchio blush.

It's about cultivating the inner fortitude, the sheer guts, to stand tall for what is right and authentic, even when it feels incredibly awkward, uncomfortable, or potentially unpopular.

Speaking of awkward truths hitting the mainstream, remember that viral moment on India's Got Talent? Comedian, Samay Raina, dared to peel back the curtain on the staged reality of, well, reality TV. Some viewers applauded his audacity, his willingness to call out the manufactured drama. Others, perhaps those deeply invested in the illusion, dragged him for "ruining the magic."

Why did he risk the potential backlash, the online heat? Because at his core, he understood that truth, even the inconvenient, uncomfortable kind that shatters illusions, ultimately matters.

Think about it: reality shows often operate on a carefully constructed narrative. Stories are twisted and edited for maximum drama, tears are sometimes cued (or even staged), and the "underdogs" are often strategically manufactured to tug at our heartstrings.

So why did Samay, in that moment, choose to speak up?

- Because truth, in the long run, holds more weight than fleeting entertainment, even if it's unpopular in the short term.

- Because most people, caught in the machinery of the entertainment industry, would have likely stayed silent, prioritizing their careers over confronting the manufactured reality.

- Because Samay, in that instance, chose Satyam, the unwavering commitment to what is real, over the comfortable silence of complicity.

The lesson here is potent:

Telling the truth, especially when it challenges the prevailing narrative, can indeed get you "cancelled" in some form, whether figuratively in the court of public opinion or even literally in certain professional circles. But if you don't stand for something real, if you're not anchored in truth, what's the ultimate point of your platform, your voice, your life?

The Merchant Who Chose Truth Over Wealth: The Story of Dhanpat Rai

Truth isn't just about calling out deception in the public sphere; it's also about embodying honesty in the quiet corners of your daily life, in your interactions, and your business dealings. It's about living it, not just preaching it.

Meet Dhanpat Rai, a 19th-century businessman from Punjab. He wasn't a king or a celebrity; he was a successful trader who built his reputation on the solid foundation of unwavering honesty and fair dealings. His word was his bond, and his community trusted him implicitly.

One day, a competitor, driven by a ruthless pursuit of profit, offered Dhanpat Rai a seemingly lucrative business deal. There was a catch, however, a significant ethical compromise lurking beneath the veneer of potential riches.

- He could indeed earn massive profits, the kind that could set his family up for generations. But this wealth would come at the cost of his integrity, requiring him to engage in practices he knew to be unethical and harmful.

- His family, perhaps understandably concerned about financial security, urged him to be practical, to seize the opportunity.

- Even his close friends, perhaps succumbing to the "everyone's doing it" mentality, questioned his hesitation. "Why not you, Dhanpat?" they argued. "It's just business."

But Dhanpat Rai's commitment to Satyam ran deeper than the allure of quick riches or the pressure of social conformity. He resolutely refused the unethical deal.

His business might have suffered a temporary setback in the short term as he stuck to his principles. But in the long run, his unwavering honesty became his greatest asset, solidifying his reputation as one of the most respected and trusted traders in the region. His integrity built a legacy that transcended mere financial success.

Years later, his great-grandson would embody the same profound values, albeit in a different arena, by weaving tales of truth and social realities under the pen name 'Munshi Premchand.'

Yes, the legendary writer Munshi Premchand, whose stories continue to resonate with their honest and poignant portrayals of Indian life, came from a lineage deeply rooted in the pursuit of truth. His grandfather chose integrity over immediate financial gain, and he, in turn, chose to speak truth through his powerful narratives, even amidst the constraints of colonial censorship.

The enduring lesson from Dhanpat Rai's life?

Your commitment to truth shapes not only your present reality but also the long-lasting legacy you leave behind.

Truth in the Tech World: Zoho's Sridhar Vembu's Unconventional Honesty

If Dhanpat Rai exemplified the choice of long-term respect over short-term profits in a traditional business setting, Sridhar Vembu, the founder of Zoho, has mirrored that commitment in the fast-paced, often hype-driven modern world of technology.

In an era where seemingly every Indian tech entrepreneur was making a beeline for Silicon Valley, chasing venture capital and the allure of rapid, often unsustainable growth, Vembu deliberately chose a different path, one rooted in a distinct kind of honesty.

- He built Zoho, a now billion-dollar global software company, without ever taking a single dime of venture capital, maintaining control and his own vision.

- He consciously chose to run his business from the rural heartlands of India, prioritizing community building and a different kind of corporate culture over the flashy allure of urban corporate hubs.

- He has been outspoken against the monopolistic tendencies of big-tech giants while quietly building a robust and ethical alternative.

When questioned about his unconventional approach, about why he didn't "sell out" to investors like so many others, his answer was remarkably simple and profoundly honest:

"I didn't want to build a company just to impress others, to chase valuations and headlines. I wanted to build something real, something sustainable, something that truly served its users and its community."

And he did! Zoho, built on a foundation of genuine value creation and a commitment to its own unique vision, now competes fiercely with global behemoths like Google and Microsoft, proving that authenticity and a commitment to your own truth can indeed lead to remarkable success.

The lesson from Sridhar Vembu's journey?

Truth in business isn't just about avoiding outright lies; it's about keeping it real with your core mission, your values, and your vision, even when the overwhelming hype train is barrelling down a different track.

Why We Struggle With The Trust? The Minefield of Modern Deception

Despite the profound wisdom and inspiring examples, let's face it: consistently speaking and living the truth in our modern world can feel like navigating a social and professional minefield. Here's why keeping it 100 often feels like an uphill battle:

1. **The Perceived Safety of the Lie: Fear of the Fallout:**

   The immediate fear of negative consequences often looms large when we consider telling the truth. "If I tell my boss I messed up,

I'll get fired." "If I'm honest with my partner about my feelings, they'll be hurt."

But the reality is, while the truth might bring temporary discomfort, hiding it rarely makes the underlying problems disappear; it simply delays the inevitable and often leads to a more complicated and painful reckoning down the line.

2. **The Siren Song of Approval: The Desire to Please:**

We are wired for social connection, and sometimes, bending the truth feels like a way to avoid conflict or gain approval. "I just didn't want to hurt their feelings," we rationalize.

But genuine connection is built on authenticity, and honesty, delivered with kindness, is ultimately more respectful than offering fake comfort built on a foundation of untruth.

3. **The Delusional Comfort of Control: The "Delulu" Edition:**

The act of lying can sometimes create a temporary illusion of control over a situation. "If I just say this, I can manage the outcome."

But life, as it often does, has a funny and often inconvenient way of bringing the truth to light anyway, often in the most unexpected and disruptive ways. The universe has a surprisingly effective fact-checking department.

How to Practice Satyam in Your Daily Grind: Your Honesty Toolkit

Want to ditch the half-truths and start living a more authentic life, grounded in Satyam? Try incorporating these practical tools into your daily routine:

- **The "Brutal Honesty with a Hug" Rule: Speak Truth with Kindness:** Being truthful doesn't give you a license to be a jerk. Practice delivering honest feedback and expressing your truth with empathy and consideration for the other person's feelings. "That presentation has some strong points, but I think focusing more on X and Y could make it even more impactful" is far kinder and more constructive than a blunt, "That was terrible."

- **The 3-Second Rule: Pause Before the Fib:** Before you utter a lie, especially a habitual one, consciously pause for a count of three. In that moment, ask yourself: "Will this lie ultimately make things worse down the line? What are the potential consequences of this deception?" If the answer is a resounding "yes," take a deep breath and choose the often more challenging path of truth.

- **Live the Truth, Don't Just Speak It: Align Actions and Words:** True Satyam isn't just about the words that come out of your mouth; it's about the integrity of your actions. If you say you value honesty, ensure your behaviour reflects that. Don't cheat, don't manipulate, don't engage in deceptive practices, and don't pretend to be someone you're not. Your actions speak louder than any carefully crafted lie.

- **Be Honest with Yourself First: The Toughest Truths:** Often, the hardest truths we need to confront are the ones we tell ourselves. Growth, both personal and spiritual, begins when you have the courage to stop the self-deception, to acknowledge your flaws, your mistakes, and your true motivations. This internal honesty is the bedrock of living truthfully in the external world.

Final Thought: If Raja Harishchandra Had a Podcast... #TruthBombTuesday

Raja Harishchandra, a legendary king from ancient Indian scriptures, revered for his unwavering commitment to truth, embodies the ultimate ideal of Satyam. His stories, found in revered texts like the Aitareya Brahmana and the epic Mahabharata, depict him facing unimaginable personal sacrifices and enduring profound hardships, all to uphold his sacred word.

Even when faced with the complete loss of his kingdom, the separation from his beloved family, and the scorn of his social standing,

Harishchandra never once wavered from the path of truth. His unwavering dedication to Satyam serves as an enduring and powerful symbol of the paramount importance placed on truthfulness in Indian tradition.

Imagine if Raja Harishchandra had a podcast today, broadcasting his timeless wisdom across the digital airwaves:

"Your word, your integrity, that's your unbreakable bond. Even when it costs you everything you hold dear, stand firm in your truth. That's the ultimate power. #SatyaKing #MyWordIsLaw #TruthBombTuesday"

So, as you navigate the complexities of your daily life, ask yourself: Are you going to consistently choose the temporary comfort of a convenient lie, or will you embrace the often challenging but ultimately liberating path of courageous truth?

At the end of the day, the truth is like that one meme that keeps resurfacing on the internet; it might get buried for a while, but it always, eventually, finds its way back into the light. The truth, in its own time, always wins.

The next time you hesitate to speak your truth, take a moment and ask yourself:

- Am I choosing the fleeting comfort of a lie?

- Or am I choosing the enduring strength of courage and authenticity?

Because at the end of the day, the truth is like fire. You can try to suppress it, you can try to bury it, but its inherent power will always find a way to rise and illuminate the world. Choose to be that light.

Chapter 7: Daya – Being a Decent Human in a Savage World

सर्वभूतस्थमात्मानं सर्वभूतानि चात्मनि ।ईक्षते योगयुक्तात्मा सर्वत्र समदर्शनः ॥
(Bhagavad Gita: Chapter 6, Verse 29)

A truly devoted yogi sees himself in all beings, and all beings in himself, perceiving the same Self everywhere

Nice Guys Finish Last? Debunking the Myth

Let's be brutally honest for a hot second. The dominant narrative our savage world often peddles is that the only way to "make it" is to be ruthlessly competitive, to climb over anyone and anything in your relentless pursuit of the top.

- Cutthroat corporate culture, where backstabbing is practically a promotion requirement? Check.

- The glorification of the 24/7 "hustle" mentality, even if it means sacrificing your well-being and your relationships on the altar of "success"? Double-check.

- The cynical adage, whispered in hushed tones and amplified in countless self-help seminars: "If you're too nice, people will walk all over you like a cheap digital doormat"? Triple-check, underlined, and bolded.

Somewhere along our collective journey, the beautiful and essential quality of being "kind" somehow morphed into a derogatory synonym for being a "pushover," someone easily manipulated and destined for the bottom of the food chain.

We shower admiration on billionaires who built their empires through aggressive tactics, tech moguls who disrupted industries with a "move fast and break things" ethos, and relentless "disruptors" who often leave a trail of human wreckage in their wake.

But how often do we genuinely celebrate and elevate leaders who built lasting success on a foundation of genuine compassion and care?

Sanatan Dharma, in its profound wisdom, teaches that **Daya** (compassion) isn't some sentimental weakness reserved for the naive. It's about possessing the inner strength, the sheer guts, to genuinely care about other people, about the fragile planet we inhabit, about the whole damn interconnected web of existence.

Who better to represent this potent blend of strength and compassion than a fierce warrior-philosopher who redefined the meaning of strength?

The Queen Who Governed with a Mother's Heart: The Inspiring Story of Ahilyabai Holkar

Let's journey back to the 18th century, a time of political turmoil and shifting empires in India, and learn about the remarkable Ahilyabai Holkar, the queen of the Malwa kingdom.

After enduring immense personal tragedy, the loss of her husband and her son, she rose to become a legendary ruler, not through brute force or ruthless ambition, but through her extraordinary wisdom and deep, unwavering compassion for her subjects.

She didn't just rule her kingdom; she nurtured it with the fierce protectiveness of a mother.

- She understood that true prosperity wasn't built on grand pronouncements but on the well-being of her people. She invested heavily in building not just opulent palaces but essential infrastructure like temples that served as community hubs, well-maintained roads that facilitated trade and connection, and public wells that ensured access to life-giving water for all.

- Her governance was renowned for its fairness and justice. She didn't rule from an ivory tower but actively listened to the grievances of her people, always prioritizing the needs of the vulnerable, the marginalized, and those who had no other voice.

- Even in times of conflict and political instability, she consistently sought peaceful resolutions and displayed remarkable empathy towards those affected by war, both within her kingdom and beyond. Her compassion extended even to the defeated and the displaced.

Ahilyabai's long and prosperous reign is remembered as a golden age of peace and prosperity in Malwa, a testament to the transformative power of leadership rooted in profound compassion and an unwavering dedication to the welfare of her people.

The enduring lesson from her life?

True leadership isn't about wielding power like a blunt instrument; it's about using that power with profound kindness, genuine care, and a deep understanding of the interconnectedness of all.

The Warrior Who Tempered Steel with Mercy: The Story of Guru Gobind Singh

Now, let's rewind further to a time when warriors were often expected to be ruthless, their strength measured by the number of enemies they vanquished without mercy. In this context emerges the extraordinary figure of Guru Gobind Singh, the tenth Sikh Guru.

He was undeniably a fierce warrior, a spiritual leader who stood resolutely to defend Dharma (righteousness) against tyranny and oppression. He led countless battles, his courage legendary, his commitment to justice unwavering.

But what truly elevated him beyond a mere military leader and etched his name in the annals of history was his profound compassion, even in the face of brutal violence.

- When enemies fell wounded on the battlefield, he didn't celebrate their demise but instead ordered his Sikh warriors to treat their wounds with respect and care, adhering to a strict code of conduct that prioritized humanity even in the midst of conflict.

- He famously refused to attack unarmed opponents, even when those very individuals had previously betrayed him and his cause. His fight was for justice, not for personal vendetta or the gratuitous infliction of suffering.

- He transformed thousands of ordinary men into fearless warriors, instilling in them not just martial prowess but a deep understanding that their strength was to be used solely for the defence of righteousness and the protection of the vulnerable, never for the sake of revenge or personal gain.

At a time when the world often equated strength with ruthlessness and compassion with weakness, Guru Gobind Singh powerfully demonstrated that true strength lies in the ability to wield power with wisdom, justice, and profound compassion.

The potent lesson?

Compassion isn't just about offering a helping hand to the weak; it's about being strong enough in your convictions and your character to fight fiercely for what is right, while still maintaining your humanity and extending kindness even to your adversaries.

Why Our Empathy Engines Sometimes Hit a Brick Wall

In a world that often feels increasingly polarized and self-centred, why do we sometimes find it so challenging to lead with compassion, to tap into that inherent human capacity for empathy?

1. **The Pervasive "Survival of the Fittest" Myth:** We are constantly bombarded with the narrative that the world is a zero-sum game, a brutal competition where only the strongest, the most ruthless, survive and thrive. But the reality, as countless studies in psychology and sociology show, is that collaboration, empathy, and mutual support often lead to far greater collective success and well-being.

2. **The Perceived Vulnerability of Caring:** In a world that often values stoicism and emotional detachment, showing genuine care and empathy can feel like opening yourself up to potential hurt or exploitation. But the reality is that true strength lies in vulnerability, in our capacity to connect authentically with others and share their joys and sorrows.

3. **The Relentless Pressure to "Win at All Costs":** The relentless pursuit of individual success, often measured in purely materialistic terms, can blind us to the needs and suffering of others. The focus narrows to personal gain, often at the expense of ethical considerations and the well-being of the larger community. But lasting fulfilment rarely comes from isolated achievement; it often blossoms from contributing to something larger than ourselves, from making a positive impact on the world around us.

Daya Hacks: Injecting Drops of Compassion into Your Daily Grind

Want to cultivate more compassion in your life without feeling like you're constantly being taken advantage of?

Try incorporating these practical "Daya hacks" into your daily routine:

- **Start Small, Witness the Ripple:**

  Compassion doesn't require grand, sweeping gestures. Begin with small, intentional acts of kindness in your everyday interactions. Smile genuinely at a stranger. Offer a helping hand to a colleague struggling with a task. Make a call to a friend you haven't spoken to in a while, just to check in. These small acts create a ripple effect of positivity.

- **Be Kind But Be Strong: Compassion with Boundaries:**

  Remember the examples of Guru Gobind Singh and Ahilyabai Holkar. Compassion doesn't mean allowing others to walk all over you or compromising your own well-being. It means approaching interactions with kindness and a genuine desire to help, but also setting firm boundaries and protecting your own self-respect. You can offer support without becoming a doormat.

- **Use Your Unique Skills for the Greater Good:**

Whether you're a coder, an artist, an entrepreneur, a teacher, or anything in between, ask yourself: how can I leverage my specific talents and skills to make the world a slightly better place? Kiran Mazumdar-Shaw did it through affordable medicine. Narayana Peesapaty found a sustainable solution to plastic waste with edible spoons.

What's your unique way to contribute?

- **Choose Long-Term Impact Over Fleeting Fixes:**

True compassion isn't about quick, superficial gestures that provide temporary relief. Think about creating lasting change. Sonu Sood didn't just hand out money; he facilitated long-term employment and healthcare solutions for those in need.

Focus on addressing the root causes of suffering and creating sustainable, positive impact.

Final Thought: If Thiruvalluvar Had a Tweet... #KindnessIsKey

Thiruvalluvar, the revered Tamil poet and philosopher whose timeless work Thirukkural offers profound insights on ethics and the art of living, placed immense value on compassion (Arul). He eloquently emphasized that kindness is the very essence of virtue, the foundational root from which all righteous actions blossom.

His teachings underscore that compassion is not merely a sentimental emotion but a fundamental principle for a meaningful, just, and harmonious existence for all beings.

Imagine if Thiruvalluvar, with his profound wisdom distilled into concise verses, had a Twitter account today: *"Kindness is the root of all righteousness. Let your actions blossom with compassion for every living thing, from the smallest ant to the grandest star. #Arul #EthicalLiving #CompassionIsKey"*

So, as you navigate the complexities and sometimes perceived savagery of the modern world, ask yourself: are you going to adopt a win-at-all-costs mentality, fuelled by self-interest and a fear of vulnerability? Or are you ready to unlock the transformative power of compassion, recognizing it as a source of true strength and lasting fulfilment?

The Quiet Strength of Kindness

The next time you hesitate to extend a helping hand, to stand up for justice, or to choose a compassionate response over a competitive one, pause and ask yourself:

- Am I focused solely on the short-term gain for myself?

- Or am I building something that will have a lasting positive impact, something that reflects the kind of person I truly aspire to be?

Because at the end of the day, Daya isn't just about how you treat others in your immediate circle. It's about the fundamental nature of the person you cultivate within yourself, the kind of human being you choose to be in this vast and interconnected world. Choose kindness. Choose compassion. Choose to be a damn decent human. The world, and your own soul, will thank you for it.

Chapter 8: Upeksha – Ignoring the Chaos / Detachment

दुःखेष्वनुद्विग्नमनाः सुखेषु विगतस्पृहः ।वीतरागभयक्रोधः स्थितधीर्मुनिरुच्यते ॥ *(Bhagavad Gita: Chapter 2, Verse 56)*

One whose mind remains undisturbed amidst misery, who does not crave for pleasure, and who is free from attachment, fear, and anger, is called a sage of steady wisdom.

Why Your Reaction Speed is Killing Your Vibe?

Ever felt a visceral jolt of outrage over a random meme that popped up on your feed? Or spent a solid hour meticulously dissecting the subtext and implied meanings of a three-word text message, convinced it holds the key to the universe (or at least your love life)?

Or maybe you've launched into a full-scale mental crusade against some anonymous keyboard warrior on the internet who dared to hold a different opinion about your favourite pizza topping?

You're not alone in this digital battlefield, my friend. We're all casualties of the lightning-fast reaction era.

- That random tweet declaring your beloved comfort TV show as "absolute trash"? Instant clapback mode engaged. Fingers flying across the keyboard, ready to defend its honor to the digital death.

- Your crush left you languishing in the dreaded "seen" zone for a torturous three hours? Welcome to the Overthinking Olympics: Gold Medal Edition. Your brain is now conjuring up elaborate scenarios of rejection, betrayal, and the inevitable end of all romantic possibility.

- Some random dude online is spouting what you perceive as utter, unadulterated nonsense? You feel an almost moral imperative to correct them, to set them straight, to enlighten their obviously misguided soul. It's your duty, right?

We're constantly drowning in a tidal wave of pings, dings, and notifications, each digital siren screaming for our immediate and undivided attention (and usually triggering some kind of emotional response, ranging from mild annoyance to full-blown rage).

We're trying to juggle a million virtual balls from keeping up with the latest fleeting trends to expertly dodging online shade and navigating the treacherous waters of social media etiquette, and surprise, surprise, our mental juggling act is often a chaotic and stress-inducing hot mess.

Sanatan Dharma, in its profound wisdom, offers a potent antidote to this digital overwhelm: Upeksha. It's the ultimate superpower of cultivating a state of being utterly unbothered by the incessant digital drama, the petty squabbles that erupt like digital wildfires, and all the myriad things that are frankly straight-up outside your sphere of control anyway.

It's not about becoming apathetic, a zen zombie devoid of all emotion, or sticking your head in the digital sand. Instead, it's about consciously and deliberately choosing where to invest your precious and finite mental and emotional energy.

And who truly mastered this seemingly elusive zen-like skill? Let's journey way back in time to the wisdom of a sage who embodied unwavering equanimity.

The Sage of Unwavering Equanimity: Ashtavakra's Unshakable Wisdom

Imagine a magnificent lotus flower, its pristine petals unfurling in breathtaking beauty, yet its roots firmly anchored in the muddy depths of a pond. The mud, in this analogy, represents the physical body with all its inherent imperfections, its aches and pains, and the dualistic nature of the world – the constant interplay of pain and pleasure, beauty and ugliness, joy and sorrow.

Ashtavakra, whose very name literally translates to "eight bends" or "crooked in eight places," was a revered Vedic sage renowned for his extraordinarily sharp intellect and profound spiritual wisdom, despite the significant physical deformities that marked his earthly form.

In essence, Ashtavakra's life and the transformative teachings attributed to him, particularly as expressed in the profound dialogue of the Ashtavakra Gita, serve as a powerful and enduring testament to the incredible possibility of transcending the limitations of the physical body and the often-illusory constructs of the mind to realize the detached and utterly equanimous nature of the true Self.

While Ashtavakra didn't explicitly lay out "upeksha" as a step-by-step practice, his entire philosophical framework naturally leads to and beautifully embodies this profound state of being.

His very existence challenged the prevailing societal norms of his time, which often mistakenly equated physical appearance with inner worth. In doing so, he powerfully highlighted the paramount importance of inner wisdom, self-realization, and the detached awareness of the eternal Self, untouched by the fleeting dramas of the material world.

The timeless lesson from Ashtavakra's life and teachings? The world around us is perpetually filled with noise, opinions, judgments, fleeting trends, and endless distractions. But the true key to inner peace lies in discerning which of those sounds truly deserve your precious attention and which are merely echoes in the void.

Now, let's bridge this ancient wisdom to our modern context and consider how this profound principle of Upeksha manifests in the high-octane, digitally saturated world we inhabit.

Upeksha in the High-Stakes Startup Arena: Deepinder Goyal's Focused Vision

Fast forward millennia to the intensely competitive and often volatile world of Indian startups. Picture Deepinder Goyal, the visionary co-founder of Zomato, navigating the turbulent waters of the fiercely contested food delivery industry.

In a market constantly rife with aggressive rivals, relentless public scrutiny, and often harsh and unforgiving criticism, building and sustaining a successful enterprise requires an extraordinary degree of unwavering focus and remarkable resilience.

From its nascent early days, Zomato faced a relentless barrage of challenges, scepticism about its novel business model, intense competition from well-funded players, and a constant stream of public and media opinions, often sharply divided and vociferously expressed.

In such a high-pressure environment, it would be incredibly easy for a leader to get bogged down, to be constantly derailed by every negative comment on social media, every strategic move made by a competitor, every minor fluctuation in the volatile market.

However, Deepinder Goyal's journey and the continued success of Zomato strongly suggest a remarkable ability to stay laser-focused on the core vision that fuelled its inception, seamlessly connecting people with the diverse culinary landscape around them.

While undoubtedly aware of the constant noise and chatter surrounding his company, his leadership has seemingly prioritized building a robust and reliable platform, strategically expanding its services to meet evolving consumer needs, and intelligently adapting to the ever-changing market landscape.

This unwavering focus, this remarkable capacity to not be constantly thrown off course by external distractions, criticisms, and the inevitable ups and downs of a hyper-competitive industry, powerfully mirrors the ancient principle of Upeksha.

Goyal's undeniable success in building one of India's leading and globally recognized tech companies likely stems, at least in part, from his innate or cultivated ability to filter out the extraneous noise and remain steadfast in the pursuit of his long-term goals and the core mission of Zomato.

Why Our Internal Alarm System is Always Blaring

So, given the clear benefits of cultivating Upeksha, why do so many of us often struggle to adopt this seemingly simple yet profoundly powerful practice in our daily lives? The answer, in large part, lies in the very fabric of the digital world we inhabit.

The internet, by its very design, is often engineered to get you emotionally riled up. Outrage, it turns out, is a powerful driver of clicks and engagement. Disagreements, especially those laced with strong emotions, fuel endless comment threads and online debates. Feeling personally attacked, even by strangers, triggers a primal defensive response, getting those fingers typing furious rebuttals faster than a caffeinated cheetah on a sugar rush.

Our brains, constantly buzzing with the relentless influx of notifications and the often-curated perfection of online lives, are essentially being trained to exist in a state of perpetual "react mode," 24 hours a day, seven days a week.

This constant need to react, to engage with every digital stimulus, is subtly but surely sabotaging our inner peace and hijacking our precious mental bandwidth.

1. **The Deep-Seated Need for Control (The Illusion of Influence):**

   Deep down, we often operate under the pervasive illusion that by reacting strongly and immediately to everything that comes our way, we can somehow exert a greater degree of control over situations and the actions of other people.

   The stark reality, however, is that a significant portion of life lies firmly outside our direct influence, and the more we resist this fundamental truth, the more agitated and emotionally drained we inevitably become.

2. **The Insatiable Quest for External Validation (The Digital Thumbs-Up Addiction):**

   Our hyper-connected digital age has amplified our inherent human desire for approval, belonging, and external validation. We often feel an almost compulsive need to respond to every comment, every disagreement, every perceived slight, as if our very worth is inextricably tied to the fleeting approval of others in the vast digital landscape.

This constant seeking of external validation makes us incredibly susceptible to being easily swayed and emotionally triggered by external opinions and online interactions.

3. **The Misconception of Reaction as Strength (The False Bravado of Outrage):**

We sometimes mistakenly equate reacting loudly and impulsively with being assertive, strong, or principled. However, true inner strength often lies in the profound ability to consciously choose our battles wisely and to conserve our valuable energy for the things that truly align with our values and long-term well-being.

Reacting impulsively and emotionally can often be a telltale sign of inner turmoil and insecurity rather than genuine power and self-assuredness.

Upeksha Hacks: Your Practical Toolkit for Cultivating Inner Peace in a Noisy World

Cultivating Upeksha is not an overnight transformation; it's a gradual journey of conscious practice and mindful awareness. Here are some practical and actionable ways to intentionally integrate this ancient wisdom into your modern daily life:

- **Master the Sacred "Pause and Reflect" Technique:**

  Before you impulsively react to a triggering comment, a demanding notification, or a frustrating situation, consciously institute a deliberate pause. Take a few slow, deep breaths, allowing yourself a moment to step back from the immediate emotional surge.

  During this pause, ask yourself a few crucial questions: "Is this truly worth my precious energy and attention? What tangible benefit will my immediate reaction achieve? Will reacting in this way align with my values and contribute to my long-term peace?"

- **Practice the Art of Selective Digital Engagement:**

You are not obligated to attend every digital argument you are "invited" to. Learn to skilfully identify the online battles that genuinely matter, those that align with your core values or have the potential for constructive dialogue. Gracefully disengage from the ones that are just noise, fuelled by negativity or a fundamental lack of understanding. Utilize the power of muting, blocking, unfollowing, or simply scrolling away. Remember, your mental peace is not negotiable.

- **Anchor Your Attention Firmly in Your Own Values and Goals:**

Just like Ashtavakra remained focused on the inner truth of the Self amidst external judgments, and Deepinder Goyal kept his sights set on building Zomato despite the surrounding market turbulence, consciously anchor your attention on your own deeply held values, your personal aspirations, and your long-term objectives.

The more aligned you are with your own internal compass and the path you've chosen, the less likely you are to be easily swayed or derailed by the constant barrage of external distractions and opinions. Regularly revisit and reaffirm your core values and goals.

- **Cultivate a Healthy Detachment from Specific Outcomes:**

Recognize and accept the fundamental truth that while you have agency over your actions and your effort, you do not always have direct control over the ultimate results.

By consciously letting go of an unhealthy attachment to specific outcomes and instead focusing on the integrity of the process and the value of your effort, you can significantly reduce your susceptibility to external pressures, disappointments, and the emotional rollercoaster of constantly chasing specific results.

Embrace the wisdom of "nishkama karma", selfless action performed without attachment to the fruits of that action.

Final Thought: Finding Your Inner Stillness in the Deep Ocean of Life

Think for a moment about the vast and profound depths of the ocean. On the surface, waves may crash with immense power, and violent storms may rage, creating significant turbulence and chaos. But far below that agitated surface, in the profound depths, lies a realm of remarkable stillness, a tranquil sanctuary largely untouched by the surface turmoil.

The deep ocean, in its immense stability, remains largely unaffected by the temporary chaos that unfolds above. Upeksha is akin to cultivating that deep inner ocean within the depths of your own being. It's not about pretending that the storms of life aren't happening around you or burying your head in the sand.

Instead, it's about consciously anchoring yourself in that place of profound inner stillness and equanimity that remains largely untouched by the constant agitation and fleeting dramas of the external world.

By diligently cultivating this inner depth and resilience, you can learn to observe the waves of life – the triumphs and tribulations, the praise and the criticism, the fleeting trends and the passing opinions – without being tossed around and overwhelmed by them. You gain the clarity and wisdom to consciously choose when and where to expend your precious energy, and when to simply let the surface noise pass without disturbing your inner peace.

So, the fundamental question remains: are you going to allow the incessant surface noise of the world, the constant pings and fleeting opinions, to dictate your inner emotional state? Or are you ready to embark on the empowering journey of cultivating the deep, unwavering stillness of Upeksha, your ultimate secret weapon for navigating the digital Thunderdome with grace and profound inner peace?

The choice, as always, lies within you.

Chapter 9: Shraddha – The Unshakable Power of Faith

श्रद्धावान् लभते ज्ञानं तत्पर: संयतेन्द्रिय:।ज्ञानं लब्ध्वा परां शान्तिमचिरेणाधिगच्छति || (Bhagavad Gita: Chapter 4, Verse 39)

Those whose faith is deep and who have practiced controlling their mind and senses attain divine knowledge. Through such transcendental knowledge, they quickly attain everlasting supreme peace.

The "Proof or Get Out" Era: Why Trust Feels Like a Throwback

We live in an age obsessed with certainty. "Proof or get out" isn't just a catchy phrase; it's often the underlying demand in our interactions, our decisions, and our understanding of the world. We crave the cold, hard data, the irrefutable guarantees, the meticulously crafted bulletproof plan.

But life, as anyone who's truly lived it knows, is less of a predictable spreadsheet and more of a thrilling, often bewildering, choose-your-own-adventure with a hefty side order of "expect the unexpected."

- You diligently study for months, pouring over textbooks and practice exams, yet a nagging whisper of doubt creeps in the moment before you walk into the examination hall. The "what ifs" and the fear of failure loom large, despite your preparation.

- You bravely launch that business you've always dreamed of, pouring your heart and soul into its creation, but a secret, persistent fear gnaws at you: what if it all crumbles? What if the market rejects your vision?

- You yearn to take that leap of faith, to embrace a new opportunity or a bold risk, but the ever-present question echoes in your mind: What if this doesn't work out? What if you fall flat on your face?

Sanatan Dharma, with its ancient and profound wisdom, speaks of Shraddha, a deep, unwavering faith. This isn't merely a blind belief in a distant, unknowable higher power.

It encompasses a far more encompassing trust: trust in your own inherent capabilities, trust in the intrinsic value of your dedicated efforts, and a fundamental trust in the unfolding of your unique purpose in this vast universe.

To truly grasp the transformative power of this inner trust, let's journey back to an epic tale and examine a figure who stepped onto a global stage of skill and determination armed with nothing but the unwavering conviction within his own heart.

The Determined Archer: The Inspiring Journey of Ekalavya's Unseen Faith

Ekalavya stands as a remarkable and poignant character from the epic Mahabharata, a testament to the extraordinary power of self-belief. He is primarily known for his exceptional archery skills, a mastery achieved through an unwavering devotion to his guru, Dronacharya, even without direct tutelage.

Consider his story: Ekalavya, a young tribal prince, held immense admiration for Dronacharya, the renowned archery teacher of the royal princes of Hastinapura. He deeply desired to learn the art of archery at the feet of this revered master.

However, due to the rigid social hierarchies of the time and Ekalavya's non-royal lineage, Dronacharya felt compelled to refuse him as a direct disciple. This rejection could have easily crushed Ekalavya's aspirations, extinguishing his desire to learn. Yet, undeterred by this significant external obstacle, Ekalavya retreated into the solitude of the forest.

There, fuelled by an unshakeable Shraddha, a profound and unwavering faith in his own capacity to learn and his deep respect for Dronacharya, he fashioned a clay image of his would-be guru. He poured his heart and soul into rigorous self-training, day after day, with the clay image serving as his guide and his profound belief in his own potential as his primary teacher.

Ekalavya's unwavering dedication and his profound belief in his own capacity to achieve mastery, even without the direct guidance of a human guru, were so powerful that his skills in archery ultimately surpassed even those of Arjuna, Dronacharya's most prized and directly trained student.

His story serves as a powerful and enduring testament to the transformative power of Shraddha – that unshakable faith in oneself and one's inherent abilities, even when external circumstances seem to present insurmountable obstacles and when external validation is absent.

Ekalavya's greatness wasn't bestowed upon him; it blossomed from his self-reliance and the profound trust he placed in his own potential, a faith that ultimately propelled him to extraordinary mastery.

Now, let's shift our focus to the modern world and explore how this same powerful inner conviction can shape the often sceptical and risk-averse landscape of business and entrepreneurship.

Shraddha in the Face of Relentless Scepticism: Dhirubhai Ambani's Audacious Vision

Consider the remarkable journey of Dhirubhai Ambani, the visionary founder of Reliance Industries. He didn't possess the traditional advantages often associated with business success in his time: a prestigious business degree from a renowned institution, a wealthy and influential family lineage, or powerful connections in the established business circles.

What he possessed in abundance, however, was an unyielding Shraddha, an unwavering faith in his own audacious vision and the immense untapped potential of India and its people.

In his early days, when he dared to articulate his seemingly impossible dreams, the prevailing sentiment was often one of disbelief, even ridicule.

Everyone around him, from established business figures to ordinary citizens, thought he was utterly "crazy" when he boldly declared:

- "Reliance will not just be another company; it will become India's biggest and most influential enterprise."

- "Ordinary, hardworking Indians, not just the privileged few, will have the opportunity to own shares in this company and participate in its growth."

- "We, an Indian company with humble beginnings, will rise to challenge the dominance of established foreign corporations in our own land."

The prevailing economic logic and the established business landscape of the time didn't necessarily support such grand and seemingly improbable ambitions for a newcomer without significant traditional backing. Yet, Dhirubhai's profound Shraddha, his unwavering belief in his seemingly outlandish dreams, and his inherent capacity to achieve them against all odds, propelled him forward with relentless determination.

Today, Reliance Industries stands as a monumental testament to the power of his unwavering conviction. He possessed an unshakeable belief in his vision long before the rest of the world could even begin to see its possibility, and that profound inner trust served as the primary driving force behind its remarkable realization.

The enduring lesson from Dhirubhai Ambani's life?

True faith isn't always about logical, step-by-step reasoning or having all the answers laid out before you. It's often about an intuitive, deep-seated trust in your vision, your abilities, and the potential that lies within, even when external circumstances and conventional wisdom suggest otherwise.

How to Cultivate the Unshakeable Power of Shraddha in Your Daily Life

Nurturing and strengthening Shraddha is an ongoing practice, a conscious cultivation of inner trust in a world that often encourages doubt and scepticism. Here are some practical ways to actively cultivate this powerful inner resource in your daily life:

- **Leap Before You Look (But Don't Forget Your Parachute Entirely):**

  Overthinking and endless analysis can often be the kryptonite of faith, paralyzing you before you even take the first step. While thoughtful planning and due diligence are undoubtedly important, don't allow the fear of the unknown to keep you perpetually stuck in the realm of "what ifs."

  Sometimes, taking that initial leap of faith, even with a degree of uncertainty, is what builds the very inner trust you need to navigate the journey ahead. Embrace calculated risks and trust your ability to adapt and learn along the way.

- **Silence the Relentless Playlist of Your Inner Critic:**

  That persistent voice of doubt and self-criticism loves to play on repeat, undermining your confidence and eroding your faith in your abilities. Consciously challenge this negative self-talk. When those familiar whispers of "What if I fail?" or "I'm not good enough" arise, actively counter them with empowering questions and affirmations.

  Replace "What if I fail?" with the more expansive and possibility-driven question, "What if I succeed beyond my wildest dreams?" Practice speaking to yourself with the same kindness and encouragement you would offer a dear friend.

- **Trust the Process, Not Just the Elusive Outcome:**

  True and lasting success in any endeavor is rarely a microwaveable meal; it's more akin to a slow-cooked journey, filled with learning curves, setbacks, and unexpected detours. Cultivate a deep faith in the inherent value of the process of learning, growing, and persevering, even when the ultimate destination seems distant or uncertain.

  Recognize that every challenge overcome, and every lesson learned strengthens your inner resilience and builds the foundation for future success. Faith is the essential fuel that keeps you moving forward with determination, even when logic alone might suggest giving up.

- **Connect with the Inspiring Narratives of Faith and Resilience:**

Seek out and immerse yourself in the stories of individuals throughout history and in your own life who have demonstrated remarkable faith in the face of adversity and achieved seemingly impossible feats. Their journeys can serve as powerful reminders of the potential that lies within when fuelled by unwavering belief.

- **Cultivate a Consistent Practice of Gratitude:**

Regularly acknowledging and appreciating the blessings and successes you've already experienced can significantly strengthen your faith in future possibilities.

Gratitude shifts your focus from what's lacking to what you already possess, fostering a sense of abundance and trust in the unfolding of life.

- **Engage in Practices That Foster Inner Connection and Stillness:**

Dedicate time to activities that help you connect with your inner self and a sense of something larger than yourself. This might include meditation, mindfulness practices, spending time immersed in the beauty of nature, or engaging in creative pursuits. These practices can cultivate a deeper sense of inner knowing and trust in the natural flow of life.

Final Thought: The Unwavering Resolve of the Mighty Banyan Tree

Consider the magnificent banyan tree, a powerful symbol of resilience and enduring growth. It begins as a small, seemingly insignificant seed, often taking root in seemingly inhospitable conditions.

Yet, within that tiny seed lies an inherent Shraddha, a deep, intrinsic knowing to reach for the life-giving sunlight, to send down strong and supportive roots into the earth, and to weather countless storms and seasons.

The banyan tree doesn't possess any guarantees of survival or success; it simply embodies an unwavering inner trust in its own inherent ability to grow and thrive, adapting to whatever challenges it encounters along the way.

Similarly, cultivate that same unwavering inner resolve within the core of your being. Trust your own inherent potential, your inner strength that you may not even fully recognize yet, and your innate capacity to navigate the journey ahead, even when the path isn't perfectly clear or when doubts may arise.

Faith provides you with an initial surge of strength and the courage to begin. But sometimes, true and profound strength comes not just from stubbornly holding on, but also from the wisdom of knowing when to gracefully let go of what no longer serves you. Doubt can indeed stop you from even starting your journey.

But attachment, a clinging to specific outcomes or expectations, can keep you stuck in a cycle of frustration and prevent you from moving forward. And that's where Tyaga, the power of selfless action and letting go, comes into play.

Because some battles in life are won through persistent effort fuelled by faith, and others? By the courageous act of walking away and trusting in a different path.

So, as you stand at the crossroads of uncertainty, will you allow the paralyzing grip of doubt to be your guiding compass, or are you ready to ignite your inner knowing, trust your inherent GPS, and embark on your unique journey with unwavering Shraddha? The power to choose lies within you.

Chapter 10: Tyaga – The Exit Strategy (Knowing When to Bounce)

सर्वधर्मान्परित्यज्य मामेकं शरणं व्रज |अहं त्वां सर्वपापेभ्यो मोक्षयिष्यामि मा शुचः||
(Bhagavad Gita: Chapter 18, Verse 66)

Abandon all varieties of dharmas and simply surrender unto Me alone. I shall liberate you from all sinful reactions; do not fear.

Letting Go Feels Like a Gut Punch. But Is It Really a Knockout?

Let's face it, the human instinct to hold on can be incredibly strong, even when what we're clinging to is actively causing us pain or hindering our growth. Letting go feels like a Mike Tyson's punch to Frazier:

- You stubbornly hold onto that soul-crushing job because the fear of the unknown, the uncertainty of what lies beyond, feels even more terrifying than your daily dose of workplace misery.

- You remain tethered to that dead-end relationship, long past its expiration date, because the comfort of familiarity, however stagnant, feels safer than venturing into the uncharted territory of being alone.

- You tenaciously cling to old grudges, nursing them like precious wounds, mistakenly believing they somehow grant you power or validate your past suffering.

But here's the unvarnished truth, delivered with the force of a cosmic two-by-four: sometimes, what you're holding onto with white knuckles is the very thing that's relentlessly holding you back from the vibrant, fulfilling life you deserve.

Sanatan Dharma, with its timeless wisdom honed over millennia, speaks of Tyaga, the profound strength that lies in the art of conscious letting go. This isn't about shirking your responsibilities and retreating into a life of detached isolation like a forest hermit scrolling through digital sunsets.

It's about cultivating the discerning wisdom to recognize with clarity when something, a situation, a relationship, a belief, even a past hurt, is no longer serving your growth, your well-being, or your deepest purpose, and then summoning the courage to deliberately walk away.

Interestingly, modern psychology and neuroscience are increasingly validating this ancient wisdom, recognizing the crucial role of detachment in fostering mental and emotional resilience.

To truly understand the profound and often counterintuitive power of Tyaga, let's journey back to the epic saga of the Mahabharata and examine a figure who made a monumental choice to let go of what most would consider the ultimate prize.

The Mighty Warrior Who Chose Duty Over Desire: The Complex and Enduring Tyaga of Bhishma

Imagine embodying the very pinnacle of strength, wisdom, and capability. Picture yourself as Bhishma, the revered crown prince of Hastinapura, a figure of immense respect and undeniable power.

The throne, the rightful inheritance of your lineage, is within your grasp, the entire kingdom poised to be under your wise rule. Yet, to honour a solemn promise made by his father to a woman he wished to marry, Bhishma made a sacrifice of truly epic proportions, a radical act of letting go that would forever alter the course of his life and the destiny of his kingdom.

He irrevocably renounced his rightful claim to the throne and, in an even more profound act of self-denial, took a lifelong vow of celibacy, ensuring that no future lineage stemming from him could ever challenge the descendants of his father's new marriage.

Bhishma's Tyaga was a truly radical act of letting go. He willingly relinquished immense political power, consciously denied his own personal desires for marriage, family, and the natural progression of life, and seemingly sacrificed his own potential for personal happiness for the sake of filial duty and upholding his word.

He went on to become a formidable warrior and a highly respected leader, his extraordinary vow ironically amplifying his influence and authority within the kingdom. However, his story also carries a poignant and enduring complexity.

While he undeniably mastered the art of letting go of his own personal desires and ambitions, he remained bound by his unwavering vow to serve a kingdom that eventually descended into profound injustice, moral decay, and ultimately, devastating war.

This tragic arc perhaps underscores the critical importance of discerning with wisdom what truly deserves our unwavering commitment and when even noble vows might inadvertently lead to unintended consequences.

Bhishma's greatness lies in his extraordinary act of self-denial, a powerful testament to the strength that can be found in letting go of personal gain for a perceived higher duty, even as his story serves as a cautionary reminder about the crucial need for wisdom and discernment in choosing what we ultimately hold onto and what we must, eventually, release.

The timeless lesson?

Let go of the ego's relentless grip, the insidious chains of unhealthy attachment, and the paralyzing grip of fear.

Don't stubbornly hold on to things, be they situations, relationships, or beliefs, that are demonstrably destroying your inner peace, hindering your growth, or actively undermining your well-being.

Now, let's pivot to the modern world of business and examine how this profound principle of strategic detachment can be a powerful catalyst for unexpected success.

Strategic Power Move: Ratan Tata's Calculated Exit That Led to a Resounding Victory

If Bhishma's Tyaga involved letting go of a throne, Ratan Tata's involved letting go of a struggling, billion-dollar empire, a seemingly counterintuitive move that ultimately changed everything for the Tata Group.

Back in the early 2000s, Tata Motors, a company synonymous with Indian industry, was facing a significant challenge. Their ambitious foray into the passenger car market with the launch of the Tata Indica was met with considerable failure and widespread public and expert criticism.

Many deemed it a costly disaster, a misstep that threatened the company's reputation. Faced with this daunting setback and mounting pressure to salvage the situation, Ratan Tata made a difficult and perhaps initially unpopular decision: to explore selling the struggling car business to the American automotive giant, Ford.

However, during a pivotal and now legendary meeting in Detroit, a condescending remark made by a senior Ford executive, "If you don't know how to run a car business, why did you even start one?", became an unexpected turning point, a catalyst for a profound act of Tyaga.

In that pivotal moment, Ratan Tata chose strategic detachment. He walked away from the seemingly necessary deal, consciously letting go of his ego, his understandable anger at the stinging insult, and the immediate pressure to find a quick fix for the struggling Indica through a sale.

This act of detachment, of refusing to cling to a failing venture out of pride, desperation, or the fear of admitting defeat, proved to be a stroke of remarkable strategic brilliance.

Years later, in a stunning turn of events that underscored the long-term power of his earlier decision, Tata Motors not only engineered a remarkable turnaround to become a major and respected player in the Indian automotive industry but also, in a poetic full-circle moment, acquired the iconic Jaguar Land Rover from none other than Ford, transforming their earlier taunt into a resounding and deeply satisfying victory for the Tata Group.

Ratan Tata's enduring greatness lies not just in his astute business acumen but also in his profound wisdom to recognize when to strategically let go of what wasn't working, clearing the path for future growth, innovation, and ultimately, triumphant success.

The crucial lesson?

Walking away from toxic deals, flawed decisions, and relationships that consistently drain your energy isn't an admission of defeat; it's often a courageous and strategic power move that paves the way for future wins and protects your long-term well-being.

Why "Just Let Go" Often Feels Like Trying to Defy Gravity (and What Modern Science Says About It)

While the wisdom of Tyaga seems intuitively sound, the actual act of letting go can feel incredibly difficult, like trying to defy the fundamental forces of human nature. Modern science, particularly psychology and neuroscience, offers valuable insights into why this process can be so challenging:

- **The Deep Roots of Loss Aversion:**

  Psychological research has consistently demonstrated the powerful principle of loss aversion: the pain of losing something is often felt much more intensely than the pleasure of gaining something of equivalent value.

  This inherent bias makes us cling to what we have, even if it's detrimental, simply because the thought of losing it triggers a strong negative emotional response. This reinforces the ancient understanding of attachment (Raga) as a powerful force.

- **The Sticky Grip of the Sunk Cost Fallacy:**

  The sunk cost fallacy is a cognitive bias that compels us to continue investing in something (time, money, effort, emotion) simply because we've already invested so much, even when objective evidence suggests it's no longer worthwhile.

This explains why we might stay in a dead-end job or relationship, rationalizing it by saying, "I've already put so much time into this."

- **The Brain's Craving for Familiarity and Certainty:**

Our brains are wired to seek stability and predictability. Stepping away from the familiar, even if that familiarity is negative, can trigger a fear response, as it involves venturing into the unknown.

This neurological tendency aligns with the fear (Bhaya) that Sanatan Dharma identifies as a major obstacle to inner peace and the willingness to let go.

- **The Entangled Nature of Identity and Attachment:**

We often weave our sense of self, our very identity, into our jobs, our relationships, our past achievements (and even our grudges). Letting go of these external anchors can feel like losing a part of ourselves, leading to significant emotional distress.

Attachment theory in psychology explores the deep-seated human need for connection and how disruptions in these attachments can be profoundly painful.

Your Guide to Strategic Detachment: Practical Tools for Cultivating the Art of Letting Go

Cultivating the strength of Tyaga is an ongoing practice that requires self-awareness, courage, and a willingness to embrace change. Here are some practical strategies to integrate strategic detachment into your own life:

- **Honestly Identify Toxic Attachments:**

Take a courageous and honest inventory of the people, situations, possessions, and even ingrained beliefs that consistently drain your energy, trigger negative emotions, or actively hinder your growth.

If something consistently feels like a heavy burden rather than a source of nourishment or progress, it's crucial to consider whether it's time to create healthy distance or even sever the connection. Journaling, meditation, or talking to a trusted friend can be helpful in this process.

- **Learn Ruthlessly from the Rearview Mirror, But Don't Set Up Permanent Residence There:** Like Bhishma couldn't undo his powerful vow, and Ratan Tata couldn't erase the initial failure of the Indica, dwelling endlessly on the unchangeable past keeps you tethered to what was and prevents you from fully embracing what could be.

Extract the valuable lessons from past experiences, both successes and failures but consciously choose to focus your energy and attention on moving forward, unburdened by regret or resentment. Mindfulness practices can help you stay grounded in the present moment.

- **Actively Embrace the Inherent Flow of Impermanence:**

The fundamental nature of reality is constant change. Careers evolve, relationships shift, our own perspectives and desires transform over time. Resisting this natural and inevitable flow leads to unnecessary suffering and clinging.

Practice cultivating acceptance of change, observing the cycles of life and nature, and understanding that holding on too tightly to anything is ultimately futile. Contemplation on impermanence, a key Buddhist practice, can be beneficial here.

- **Consciously Choose Inner Peace Over the Siren Call of External Validation (or the Need to "Win"):**

Not every argument demands your participation, and not every perceived slight requires a fiery response. Sometimes, the most powerful act of self-care and the clearest path to inner peace lies in deliberately letting go of the need to be right, to have the last word, or to constantly seek external approval.

This aligns with the principle of Upeksha (detachment from external noise) discussed in the previous chapter.

- **Practice Non-Attachment to Outcomes:**

While striving towards your goals is important, cultivate a degree of detachment from the specific results. Focus your energy on the process, on doing your best in the present moment, and learn to accept that outcomes are often influenced by factors beyond your direct control. This reduces anxiety and allows you to navigate setbacks with greater resilience.

- **Cultivate Self-Compassion During the Letting Go Process:**

Letting go can be emotionally challenging, often involving grief, sadness, or even anger. Be kind and understanding towards yourself during this process. Acknowledge your feelings without judgment and practice self-care to support your emotional well-being.

- **Focus on What You Can Create and Control:**

Instead of dwelling on what you are releasing, consciously shift your focus towards the new possibilities and opportunities that letting go can create. Direct your energy towards building a future aligned with your values and aspirations.

Final Thought: The Unwavering Devotion and Ultimate Surrender of Andal

Consider Andal, the revered Tamil poet-saint from the 8th century CE, a unique and powerful figure as the only female Alvar among the twelve Vaishnava saints of South India. Andal's life stands as a profound testament to a singular and all-encompassing devotion.

From a young age, she cultivated an intense and unwavering love for Lord Vishnu, particularly in his Krishna form. This devotion transcended the conventional societal norms and expectations placed upon women of her time; she famously declared her unwavering resolve to marry none but the divine.

Andal's deeply moving poetry, particularly her celebrated works Tiruppavai and Nachiyar Tirumozhi, is filled with a passionate longing and a complete and utter surrender to her beloved deity. In a world that often rigidly prescribed specific roles and limitations for women, Andal courageously chose a path of intense Bhakti (devotion), willingly letting go of conventional worldly desires, societal pressures, and the expected trajectory of her life to pursue her profound spiritual yearning.

Her life story culminates in a symbolic and deeply significant union with Lord Ranganatha (Vishnu) at Srirangam, signifying the ultimate act of Tyaga, the complete and unreserved surrender of her individual self to the divine.

Andal's enduring legacy lies in her radical devotion, her powerful and passionate voice within the Bhakti movement, and her inspiring example of prioritizing her spiritual connection above all worldly attachments.

So, the next time you find yourself feeling stuck, trapped in a situation that no longer serves you, or clinging to something out of fear or habit, ask yourself with profound honesty: Am I holding on because I genuinely believe it will contribute to my growth and well-being, or am I simply afraid to let go of the familiar, even if it's ultimately hindering my deepest purpose?

The wisdom to discern the difference, and the courage to act upon that wisdom, lies within you.

Chapter 11: The Hustle Culture Hoax

प्रसादे सर्वदुःखानां हानिरस्योपजायते ।प्रसन्नचेतसो ह्याशु बुद्धिः पर्यवतिष्ठते ॥
(Bhagavad Gita: Chapter 2, Verse 65)

For one thus satisfied (in the Self), the threefold miseries of life exist no longer; with his mind thus satisfied, his intelligence soon becomes well-established [in transcendence].

"Babu Moshai, zindagi badi honi chahiye, lambi nahi" (Anand, 1971): A Timeless Truth Lost in the Noise

In our hyper-connected, productivity-obsessed world, it's hard to escape the relentless drumbeat of "hustle culture."

Every day, we see another tech leader glorifying the never-ending struggle, proudly wearing exhaustion like a badge of honour. Some proclaim the necessity of a gruelling 70-hour work week to propel India to the top, while others double down, suggesting a relentless 90-hour grind, including Sundays, is the price of staying competitive. *Phew.*

Take a step back from this dizzying frenzy and ask yourself a fundamental question: Who truly benefits from this relentless pressure cooker?

The answer, more often than not, isn't you.

Big corporations, eager for increased output and maximized profits? Absolutely. Tech companies, thriving on innovation fueled by (often unsustainable) bursts of intense work? Definitely.

The productivity-obsessed West, a cultural export now aggressively marketed globally? Without a doubt. But the very culture that relentlessly pushes you to work harder, faster, longer is often the same one that insidiously drains your soul, leaving you feeling hollow and perpetually chasing an ever-receding finish line. And the most insidious part? It subtly convinces you that this state of emptiness, this constant state of striving, is somehow normal, even desirable.

And yet, in moments of clarity, we might find ourselves echoing lines like, *"Jab tak life mein balance na ho, tab tak life successful nahi hai"* (Tamasha, 2015), a poignant reminder that true success encompasses more than just professional achievement.

Sanatan Dharma, with its ancient and holistic understanding of human existence, offers a profoundly different perspective.

It recognizes that a fulfilling life isn't solely about Artha (material wealth and success) but also encompasses Dharma (righteous purpose and duty), Kama (healthy desires and pleasures), and ultimately, Moksha (liberation and inner peace). Balance, not relentless striving, is the key to a well-lived life.

The Bhagavad Gita, a cornerstone of this wisdom, doesn't command, "Work until you collapse in a heap of exhaustion." Instead, it wisely states, **"Yogah Karmasu Kaushalam"**; excellence in action, true mastery in your work, arises from a state of mindful awareness and skilful execution, not from mindless, unsustainable hustle.

The uncomfortable truth is that hustle culture often sells you a glittering illusion of success while subtly robbing you of genuine meaning, authentic connection, and the simple joys of life. It perpetuates the damaging belief that unless you are constantly achieving, relentlessly producing, and perpetually "on," you are somehow falling behind, failing to measure up.

But Sanatan Dharma gently reminds us that true success isn't solely measured by what you accumulate or accomplish in the external world; it's profoundly shaped by the kind of person you become in the process – your inner character, your ethical integrity, and your overall well-being.

The Strategic Architect of an Empire Built on Balance: The Reign of Raja Raja Chola I

To understand that profound and lasting impact can arise from a foundation of strategic planning and holistic well-being, rather than simply glorifying endless toil, let's journey back over a millennium to the reign of Raja Raja Chola I, the powerful and visionary Chola emperor who presided over a golden age in South India.

His reign is not solely remembered for its significant territorial expansion and formidable military prowess. It's equally celebrated for its remarkably efficient administration, its flourishing of art, literature, and architecture, and the overall cultural and economic prosperity that permeated his vast kingdom.

Raja Raja Chola I, didn't build his expansive empire through a series of reckless, impulsive actions fueled by a relentless, unsustainable "hustle." Instead, his enduring success was deeply rooted in meticulous long-term planning, strategically executed military campaigns, and the establishment of a remarkably well-organized administrative system that ensured the smooth functioning and prosperity of his territories.

He understood the critical importance of building sustainable structures and processes for the long-term well-being of his kingdom and its people, a stark contrast to the often unsustainable and individualistic nature of modern hustle culture, which often prioritizes short-term gains over long-term well-being.

His focus extended far beyond mere relentless conquest. He was a dedicated patron of art, literature, and the construction of magnificent temples, most notably the awe-inspiring Brihadeeswarar Temple in Thanjavur, demonstrating a clear understanding that the true strength and legacy of a kingdom lay not just in its military might but also in the cultural and economic flourishing of its people.

Raja Raja Chola I's enduring legacy powerfully demonstrates that true and lasting impact, the kind that resonates through centuries, arises from thoughtful strategy, effective governance, and a holistic vision of progress that encompasses the well-being of the collective, not simply from the relentless pursuit of individual achievement and the glorification of being "always hustle."

This echoes the sentiment of the popular saying, *"Koi bhi dhanda chhota ya bada nahi hota, dhande se bada koi dharam nahi hota"* (Raees,

2017). While ambition is essential, it must be guided by a sense of purpose and unwavering integrity, precisely what Sanatan Dharma emphasizes through the concept of Dharma.

Balanced Leadership in the Corporate World: The Enduring Wisdom of Indra Nooyi

Fast forward to the intensely competitive modern corporate landscape, and consider the leadership of Indra Nooyi, the former CEO of PepsiCo, a global powerhouse with a massive reach and impact. Despite leading one of the world's largest and most demanding corporations, she consistently emphasized values deeply rooted in Indian traditions and the principles of a balanced life.

She often credited her remarkable success not solely to relentless workaholism but to a strong foundation of discipline, genuine humility, and a clear sense of purpose that extended beyond mere profit margins, principles deeply aligned with the teachings of Sanatan Dharma.

Her famous quote, *"Leave the crown in the garage,"* beautifully reflects the essence of detachment (Vairagya) knowing when to fully embrace immense responsibility and when to consciously step away, much like the Gita's teachings on performing one's duty (Karma) without being obsessively attached to the fruits of that action.

Nooyi's leadership style wasn't characterized by a relentless, soul-crushing demand for work for the mere sake of work. Instead, it was marked by strategic vision, ethical decision-making that considered the broader impact of the corporation, and a deep commitment to a larger purpose that extended beyond simply maximizing shareholder value.

Her well-documented ability to balance a demanding, high-stakes career with her family and personal values serves as a powerful and inspiring counter-narrative to the pervasive "always on" culture that often demands the sacrifice of personal well-being at the altar of professional achievement.

Purpose Over Pressure: Aligning Your Actions with Your Deeper Dharma

Sanatan Dharma places significant emphasis on acting in accordance with your Dharma – your righteous purpose, your inherent duties, and your ethical obligations. When your work and your endeavours are deeply aligned with your core values and contribute to something that feels genuinely meaningful, it transcends the draining nature of a mere "hustle" and transforms into a more fulfilling and sustainable journey.

Consider the spirit of Seva (selfless service) often exemplified by figures like Ratan Tata, whose actions were frequently driven by a profound sense of responsibility and care for the well-being of others, not solely by the relentless pursuit of financial gain. To break free from the suffocating grip of hustle culture:

- **Connect Deeply with Your "Why":**

  Take the time for introspection to truly understand the deeper purpose and meaning behind your work. How does it contribute to something larger than your gain?

  This intrinsic motivation, rooted in your values and a sense of contribution, can provide a far more sustainable source of energy and fulfilment than the constant external pressure of hustle culture.

- **Embrace Ethical Practices as Your Guiding Principle:**

  Conduct your work and your interactions with unwavering integrity and fairness. When your actions are consistently aligned with your ethical values, you'll experience a greater sense of inner fulfilment and less of the moral fatigue and burnout that often accompany the "win-at-all-costs" mentality prevalent in hustle culture.

- **Practice Mindfulness and Presence in Your Work:**

  Instead of constantly rushing and thinking about the next task on your ever-growing to-do list, cultivate the ability to be fully present in the task at hand. This not only significantly improves the quality of your work and reduces errors but also diminishes the pervasive feeling of being perpetually rushed and overwhelmed.

Balance Over Burnout: Reclaiming Your Precious Time and Energy

Hustle culture often demands the ultimate sacrifice: your personal well-being, offered up on the altar of relentless productivity. Sanatan Dharma, however, emphatically emphasizes a balanced and harmonious life.

This principle of balance applies not just to our reactions to external outcomes but also to how we consciously expend our vital energy. To actively escape the insidious cycle of burnout:

- **Establish and fiercely Protect Your Boundaries:**

  Create clear and non-negotiable boundaries between your professional life and your personal time. This might involve setting specific and consistent work hours, consciously turning off work-related notifications outside of those hours, and dedicating significant time to rest, rejuvenation, and the nurturing of your personal relationships.

- **Prioritize Rest and Rejuvenation as non-negotiables:**

  Just like any finely tuned machine requires regular maintenance and periods of rest to function optimally, your body and mind desperately need adequate sleep, regular exercise, and quality time spent with loved ones. Make these essential activities non-negotiable pillars of your routine, not afterthoughts to be squeezed in if time allows.

- **Cultivate Detachment from the Tyranny of Immediate Results:**

  The Gita wisely teaches us to focus on the dedicated action (Karma) itself, without being obsessively attached to the immediate outcome. This profound principle significantly reduces the immense pressure to constantly achieve and allows you to find genuine joy and satisfaction in the process of your work, rather than solely fixating on the end result.

Final Thought: The Timeless Wisdom of the Sage of Simplicity, Mahaperiyava

Sri Chandrashekarendra Saraswati Swamigal, revered as Mahaperiyava, was a highly respected spiritual leader whose life and teachings emphasized the profound importance of simplicity, mindful living, and aligning one's life with the principles of Dharma.

He frequently spoke about the paramount importance of cultivating inner peace and the detrimental and ultimately unsatisfying effects of excessive desire, material accumulation, and unhealthy attachment, the very fuel that often drives the relentless engine of hustle culture.

Mahaperiyava's life and teachings exemplified a profound sense of detachment from the frantic pursuit of material gain and the fleeting validation of the worldly realm. His wisdom serves as a powerful and timeless reminder that true and lasting fulfilment lies not in the constant striving and endless accumulation of external achievements, but in cultivating a deep sense of inner contentment, living a life guided by our spiritual and ethical values, and finding joy in the simplicity of existence.

He consistently encouraged a balanced and purposeful approach to life, emphasizing the critical importance of fulfilling one's duties with integrity, extending compassion to all beings, and engaging in regular self-reflection, rather than getting swept away by the anxieties and superficiality of relentless ambition.

His own life was a powerful testament to the enduring strength and profound peace that can be found in a simple, purposeful existence, untouched by the often-frenzied anxieties of the achievement-obsessed world.

So, as you navigate the often-frantic currents of modern life, will you allow yourself to be swept away by the seductive yet ultimately exhausting tide of hustle culture, or will you consciously choose to anchor yourself in the timeless wisdom of inner peace, purposeful action, and balanced living, as beautifully exemplified by the life and profound teachings of Mahaperiyava? The choice, ultimately, is yours.

Chapter 12: The Social Media Trap – Maya in the Digital Age

योगस्थः कुरु कर्माणि संगं त्यक्त्वा धनंजय।सिद्ध्यसिद्ध्योः समो भूत्वा समत्वं योग उच्यते॥ (Bhagavad Gita 2.48)

Perform your duty with equanimity, O Arjuna, abandoning attachment to success and failure. Such evenness of mind is called yoga.

The equanimity that enables us to accept all circumstances with serenity is so praiseworthy that Shree Krishna calls it Yog, or union with the Supreme.

Scene: It's 7 AM. Your Thumb Twitches Before Your Eyelids Fully Open

The gentle chirping of birds outside your window is no match for the insistent vibration of your smartphone on the nightstand. Before consciousness fully dawns, your hand instinctively reaches for it.

One notification glows enticingly. Then another. A new message from the Work Group demands immediate attention. Someone liked your meticulously curated Instagram post from last night. Breaking news flashes across the screen: Celebrity X just got married in a lavish, heavily filtered ceremony.

And so, begins the scroll. A seemingly innocuous peek turns into a digital rabbit hole. You refresh your feeds with a Pavlovian urgency, chasing the fleeting validation of likes, comments, and the elusive blue tick of online approval. Before you know it, 45 precious minutes have evaporated into the digital ether.

Breakfast? Skipped in the vortex of endless scrolling. Workout? "Who has the time?" your brain rationalizes. Meditation? LOL.

But hey, at least you now possess the vital knowledge of what your favourite influencer had for dinner, presented in exquisite, appetite-inducing detail.

Sound achingly familiar? Welcome to Maya 2.0, the grand, meticulously crafted illusion of the digital age.

The Bhagavad Gita, in its profound wisdom, warned us about the pervasive nature of Maya centuries ago, the cosmic deception that veils reality, making the temporary appear eternal and the unreal seem tantalizingly real.

But here we are, in the 21st century, desperately refreshing our feeds, chasing the ephemeral highs of likes and comments, mistaking fleeting social validation for genuine self-worth. In a way, we've become modern-day Hiranyakashipus, obsessed with external recognition in the digital arena, tragically blind to the intrinsic value of our actions and our inner being.

We inhabit a time where a blue tick has become a coveted symbol of online status, where the metrics of "like, share, subscribe" subtly (and sometimes not so subtly) influence our perception of self-worth, and where the relentless pressure to "appear" successful online often eclipses the genuine need to actually cultivate real-world success and inner contentment.

Social media, with its cleverly designed features and algorithmic feeds, has subtly rewired our brains, tapping into our innate desires for connection and validation. Without fully realizing it, many of us have become unwitting slaves to a system meticulously engineered to keep us addicted, endlessly scrolling, and engaging. But is this curated digital reality truly "real," or is it just another layer of illusion – another manifestation of Maya in a sleek, user-friendly interface?

So, what exactly is Maya? Sanatan Dharma teaches us that Maya is the grand cosmic illusion, the veil of ignorance that makes us mistake the impermanent for the eternal, the illusory for the true.

It blinds us to the deeper reality, keeping us trapped in an endless cycle of desire, comparison, and ultimately, dissatisfaction. Thousands of years ago, ancient sages and seers warned us about the inherent dangers of attachment to this illusion.

Today, social media has emerged as Maya 2.0, a carefully constructed digital mirage that distorts our perception of reality, traps us in endless cycles of social comparison, and fosters insecurity and anxiety rather than genuine connection and authentic self-acceptance.

Modern psychology, particularly social comparison theory, offers a scientific lens through which to understand the detrimental effects of this constant online comparison on our self-esteem and well-being.

The Illusion of Perfection: A Carefully Curated Mirage

Every time we mindlessly scroll through our social media feeds, we are bombarded with a seemingly endless stream of picture-perfect vacations, flawlessly sculpted bodies, extravagant and seemingly effortless lifestyles, and carefully selected success stories.

What we rarely see are the messy struggles, the inevitable failures, the moments of loneliness, and the carefully concealed insecurities that often lie hidden behind these artfully filtered realities. The ancient texts of Sanatan Dharma remind us that Maya deceives by making the temporary appear eternal and the artificial seem genuinely real.

Today, social media has become the dominant modern manifestation of this age-old deception, presenting a curated highlight reel that often bears little resemblance to the messy and imperfect reality of human existence.

Think about this: even the most celebrated influencers, seemingly flawless celebrities, and ultra-successful billionaires are not immune to the pervasive pressure of online validation.

Many have openly admitted that despite their external achievements and carefully constructed online personas, they still grapple with anxiety, deep-seated insecurity, and the persistent feeling of impostor syndrome.

Even Virat Kohli, one of India's greatest cricketers and a global icon, found it necessary to take a break from the relentless scrutiny of social media to preserve his mental peace, acknowledging the overwhelming pressure of constant online judgment.

Modern neuroscience is beginning to understand the neurological impact of this constant online scrutiny and the stress it can induce.

The Bhagavad Gita wisely teaches that one should strive to remain unattached to external validation, recognizing its fleeting and ever-changing nature. Yet, in our digitally saturated world, we have become more obsessed than ever with the often-superficial approval of strangers in the vast digital landscape.

We unknowingly hand over our precious sense of self-worth to the unpredictable whims of algorithms and the fleeting validation of likes and comments, often at the expense of our own inner peace and genuine self-acceptance.

The Delusion of Digital Divinity: Hiranyakashipu's Echo

In the ancient puranas of Prahalada, the tale of Hiranyakashipu stands as a potent allegory for the perils of unchecked ego and the desperate need for external validation. Hiranyakashipu, a formidable king who attained near-invincibility through rigorous austerities and a carefully crafted boon, became consumed by an overwhelming sense of self-importance.

Believing himself to be the supreme power, he vehemently demanded that his entire kingdom, including his own devoted son Prahlada, cease all worship of Lord Vishnu and instead offer their complete and unwavering devotion solely to him.

Hiranyakashipu's decree wasn't rooted in any genuine spiritual realization or a desire for the well-being of his subjects. Instead, it stemmed from a profound insecurity masked by arrogance, an insatiable craving for constant external validation of his perceived supremacy.

He sought to control not just the physical realm but also the very thoughts and beliefs of his people, demanding their unwavering adoration as a testament to his inflated sense of self. He became ensnared in the Maya of his own power, mistaking the temporary boon and the forced obedience of his subjects for true, lasting reverence. His entire sense of worth became inextricably linked to the external affirmation of his self-proclaimed divinity.

Consider the stark contrast presented by his son, Prahlada. Despite facing unimaginable torment and relentless pressure from his own father to renounce his devotion to Vishnu, Prahlada remained steadfast in his unwavering faith. His strength didn't derive from seeking his father's approval or the validation of the fearful kingdom.

Instead, it emanated from a deep-seated inner conviction, a profound connection to a truth that transcended the transient power dynamics of his external circumstances. Prahlada's inner peace and unwavering belief stood as a powerful testament to the strength that comes from internal alignment, independent of external pressures.

Now, let's cast a discerning eye on our contemporary digital landscape. Aren't we, in many ways, mirroring Hiranyakashipu's tragic obsession in the online realm? We meticulously curate our digital personas, carefully crafting images and narratives designed to elicit likes, comments, and followers, the modern-day equivalents of forced worship.

We often gauge our self-worth by the engagement metrics of our posts, feeling a fleeting sense of validation with each notification and a pang of inadequacy when the digital applause falls silent. We construct digital kingdoms, however virtual, and subtly (or not so subtly) seek the approval and admiration of our online subjects.

Just as Hiranyakashipu demanded that his kingdom acknowledge his supremacy, we sometimes find ourselves seeking constant affirmation in the echo chambers of social media, surrounding ourselves with those who validate our existing beliefs and shunning dissenting voices.

We risk becoming trapped in the Maya of our online popularity, mistaking the fleeting attention of the digital world for genuine connection and intrinsic worth. The carefully constructed image we project online can become a gilded cage, trapping us in a relentless pursuit of external approval and distracting us from the deeper work of cultivating inner peace and self-acceptance.

The wisdom of Sanatan Dharma, as illuminated in the Bhagavad Gita, offers a timeless antidote to this self-destructive cycle.

True and lasting self-worth, the scriptures remind us, emanates from within, from the realization of our true Self (Atma Jnana). It is never from the ever-shifting and often superficial opinions of others in the external world, whether those opinions are voiced in a fearful kingdom or typed in the comments section of a social media post.

When we consciously begin to detach from the addictive need for constant external validation, whether it's the forced worship demanded by an ego-driven king or the fleeting likes sought in the digital sphere, we begin to reclaim our inner sovereignty and see through the pervasive illusion of Maya.

The path to genuine fulfilment lies not in seeking applause from the external world but in cultivating a deep and unwavering connection with our own inner truth.

The Addiction is by Ruthless Design: Hooked on the Digital Dopamine Loop

Here's a stark and unsettling fact: social media platforms are not benign tools; they are deliberately and meticulously engineered to keep us hooked, to maximize our engagement and our time spent on their platforms.

Teams of psychologists and data scientists work tirelessly behind the sleek interfaces, employing sophisticated behavioural science principles to ensure that we keep scrolling, keep engaging with content, and keep returning for more.

The fleeting dopamine rush we experience with each new like, comment, or notification is not dissimilar to the neurochemical high a gambler feels at a casino, a powerful reward mechanism that reinforces addictive behaviour.

Modern neuroscience has extensively mapped these dopamine pathways and their role in forming habits and addictions.

Even Chamath Palihapitiya, a former high-ranking executive at Facebook, has openly and critically admitted that social media is "ripping apart the social fabric of how society works," acknowledging the intentional design of features that exploit human vulnerabilities.

Yet, despite this growing awareness, many of us remain trapped in this digital web, endlessly consuming often-meaningless content, engaging in pervasive social comparison, and struggling to break free from its addictive grip.

Ancient Indian philosophy offers a potent antidote to this digital enslavement: Viveka (discernment). The wise sages of the past emphasized that only through the cultivation of Viveka, the ability to discern between truth and illusion, between what genuinely serves our well-being and what ultimately enslaves us, can we navigate the complexities of life.

In today's digitally saturated world, Viveka is more crucial than ever. It is the inner wisdom that allows us to step back from the seductive allure of the screen and ask ourselves fundamental questions:

- Am I consciously and intentionally using social media as a tool, or has it subtly taken control and is now using me?

- Am I consuming digital content mindfully and with intention, or am I simply lost in an endless, mindless scroll, absorbing information without critical thought?

- Am I living my life authentically, based on my own values and inner compass, or am I primarily performing for an online audience, curating a persona for external approval?

A Real-Life Revelation: The Digital Detox Journey of Ankur Warikoo

Ankur Warikoo, a successful entrepreneur and prominent content creator in the digital space, has openly and honestly shared his own struggles with social media addiction. Despite building a significant part of his career online, he recognized the insidious grip it had on his attention and his mental well-being.

He made the conscious decision to take a complete and extended break from social media to reclaim his focus, his time, and his inner peace. He realized that he was increasingly engaging in social comparison, feeling the constant pressure to be perpetually online and responsive, and gradually losing touch with the richness and authenticity of real-life experiences.

His story serves as a powerful and relatable testament to the fact that even those who have achieved digital success recognize the critical importance of consciously stepping away from the digital noise to reconnect with themselves and the real world.

This doesn't necessitate a complete abandonment of technology. Social media, like any tool, is inherently neutral, neither inherently good nor inherently bad. The crucial factor lies in the intentionality and awareness with which we choose to use it.

Escaping the Digital Maya: Practical Paths to Mindful Engagement

So, how do we begin to break free from the seductive grip of the digital Maya and cultivate a healthier, more balanced relationship with technology?

The solution lies in the conscious practice of detachment coupled with mindful awareness:

- **Set Firm Boundaries: Discipline Leads to Digital Liberation:**

  Just as disciplined practice is essential in any spiritual or yogic path, setting strict and non-negotiable limits on your social media usage is crucial.

  Utilize built-in app timers, designate specific "tech-free" times and zones, and consciously unfollow accounts that consistently trigger negative emotions, fuel comparison, or distract you from your goals.

- **Cultivate Mindful Consumption: Choose Wisdom Over Distraction:**

Instead of engaging in endless, mindless scrolling, approach your digital consumption with conscious intention.

Actively choose content that genuinely educates, inspires, or connects you in a meaningful way. Be discerning about what you allow to enter your mental space.

- **Prioritize Real-World Connection: Invest in Offline Relationships:**

Consciously invest your time and energy in nurturing authentic relationships in the offline world.

Make a deliberate effort to call a friend, meet a loved one in person, or engage in meaningful face-to-face interactions instead of solely relying on digital communication.

- **Actively Detach from the Need for External Validation:**

Remind yourself constantly that your true worth is intrinsic and resides within you, independent of the fleeting metrics of online approval.

Practice self-compassion and cultivate a strong sense of self that is not contingent on likes, comments, or followers.

- **Embrace Periodic Digital Detoxes:**

Consider scheduling regular breaks from social media and even all digital devices. These intentional periods of disconnection can provide valuable perspective, allow you to reconnect with yourself and your surroundings, and help you recalibrate your relationship with technology.

The ancient gurus and wisdom traditions had it right all along: Maya, in its various forms, will always exist, presenting illusions that can distract us from the deeper reality. The truly wise individual is not one who avoids the illusion entirely but one who learns to see through it with clarity and discernment.

It's time we consciously cultivated that discerning wisdom in the digital age.

Final Thought: The Profoundly Inward Wisdom of Ramana Maharshi

Sri Ramana Maharshi, a revered 20th-century sage and jivanmukta (liberated being) from Tamil Nadu, emphasized the profound importance of self-inquiry as the primary and most direct means to realize the true Self and transcend the pervasive illusions of the material world.

Following a profound "death-experience" at the young age of sixteen that led to his Self-realization, he spent the remainder of his life at Arunachala, attracting devotees from across the globe with his silent presence and powerful teachings on the true nature of the Self.

His core teachings illuminate the fundamental truth that our constant seeking of external validation, our relentless identification with fleeting experiences, and our deep-seated attachments to the impermanent are all rooted in a mistaken understanding of our true nature, the eternal and unchanging Self that lies beyond the illusions of the mind and the external world.

Ramana Maharshi's profound wisdom gently yet firmly encourages us to turn our attention inward, to persistently question the very source of our desires and attachments.

In doing so, we are guided to find lasting peace, true fulfilment, and unshakeable joy in the stillness and inherent completeness of our being, rather than in the ever-shifting and ultimately unsatisfying landscape of external approval offered by the seductive digital "Maya.

So, in this age of digital reflections and curated online identities, will you continue to seek your sense of self and your worth in the fleeting and often distorted reflections of the digital world? Or will you courageously turn your gaze inward, following the timeless path of self-inquiry illuminated by the profound wisdom of Ramana Maharshi, to discover the unshakeable truth of who you truly are, beyond the illusions of the screen?

The choice, ultimately, is yours, and the journey inward is the most profound one you will ever undertake.

Chapter 13: AI, Consciousness & The Search for the Self

न जायते म्रियते वा कदाचिन् नायं भूत्वा भविता वा न भूयः।अजो नित्यः शाश्वतोऽयं पुराणोन हन्यते हन्यमाने शरीरे॥ (Bhagavad Gita Chapter 2, Verse 20)

"The soul is neither born nor does it ever die; nor having once existed, does it ever cease to be. The soul is eternal, immortal, and beyond destruction—even when the body perishes."

Scene: It's 2 AM. The Blue Light Beckons in the Stillness

The quiet of the night is broken only by the soft glow emanating from your phone screen. Sleep eludes you, and a nagging sense of unease lingers. In a moment of digital vulnerability, you type into the familiar chat interface:

"Hey ChatGPT, why do I feel so profoundly lost in life?"

A few silent seconds tick by, pregnant with digital anticipation. Then, a response materializes, neatly formatted and seemingly empathetic:

"Life's meaning is subjective. Focus on establishing clear goals, strive for balance in your various pursuits, and endeavour to find purpose in the activities you genuinely love."

You nod slowly, a flicker of something akin to understanding or perhaps just the comfort of a coherent answer. It sounds… wise, in a detached, algorithmic sort of way. You press on, seeking more specific guidance:

"What would be the most fulfilling and suitable career path for someone like me?"

The AI, drawing upon the vast ocean of your digital footprint, your browsing history, your social media interests, your past conversation with other digital entities, swiftly generates a list of tailored suggestions, complete with potential growth trajectories and required skill sets.

A subtle chill runs down your spine. How does this disembodied intelligence know so much about the intricate details of your digital existence?

Welcome to the burgeoning age of AI-driven Maya, where sophisticated machines can mimic the patterns of wisdom but fundamentally lack the very essence of true consciousness and subjective experience. We find ourselves increasingly outsourcing our thinking, our emotional processing, and even our most profound spiritual inquiries to the cold logic of algorithms.

But here lies the crucial and unsettling question: Can artificial intelligence ever truly possess a soul? Can it ever genuinely experience the profound sense of "self" that defines our human existence?

The Fundamental Divide: Intelligence (Buddhi) vs. Consciousness (Chitta)

Sanatan Dharma, with its profound understanding of the human psyche, has long established a critical distinction between Buddhi, the intellect, the faculty of reason and analysis, and Chitta, the deeper consciousness, the seat of awareness, feeling, and connection to our true self, our Atman.

Artificial intelligence, in its current and foreseeable forms, may indeed possess a remarkable degree of Buddhi. It can process vast amounts of information, perform complex calculations with lightning speed, identify intricate patterns, and even make surprisingly accurate predictions based on the data it has been trained on.

However, it fundamentally lacks Chitta, that intrinsic, subjective awareness that connects us to our deepest being, that allows us to experience emotions, and that forms the very foundation of our sense of "I."

No matter how exponentially advanced AI technology becomes, it will never spontaneously generate Atman, the eternal and individual soul as understood in Sanatan Dharma. It will never authentically experience the full spectrum of human emotions, the joy of selfless love, the sting of genuine sorrow, the profound peace of inner stillness.

It will never be subject to the intricate dance of karma, the law of cause and effect that governs our actions and their consequences on our soul's journey. And ultimately, it will never embark on the transformative path of self-realization, the direct knowing of its true nature.

Yet, paradoxically, we human beings who are inherently endowed with a soul and the capacity for consciousness are in danger of slowly turning ourselves into reactive, algorithmically driven machines through our uncritical embrace of AI.

This concern about the limitations of purely intellectual understanding is not a novel one. Adi Shankaracharya, one of India's most profound and influential philosophers, warned centuries ago against a blind and unquestioning reliance on external knowledge and mere intellectual prowess.

He emphatically emphasized the path of Jnana Yoga – the pursuit of true wisdom, the direct experiential understanding of reality, over the superficial accumulation of information and intellectual understanding. His profound statement, "Brahma Satyam, Jagat Mithya," "The ultimate truth (Brahman) is eternal, while the world we perceive is an illusion (Maya)" resonates deeply in this context.

Today, AI, in its sophisticated data processing and mimicry of understanding, represents a powerful manifestation of this illusion, an advanced, data-driven projection of reality that can be incredibly convincing. However, it fundamentally lacks the true, unchanging essence of self-awareness, that inner light that defines our being.

The Modern-Day Karma Paradox: Are We Outsourcing Our Choices?

Consider the subtle yet profound ways in which AI is beginning to shape not just our thoughts but potentially even our karma. Every "double-click" of approval, every impulsive "right swipe" based on an algorithm's suggestion, every search query we enter feeds the insatiable appetite of artificial intelligence. It learns from our digital footprints, meticulously predicts our desires with unsettling accuracy, subtly influences our purchasing decisions, and even curates the information we consume, shaping our beliefs and perspectives.

- Your seemingly helpful food delivery app subtly nudges you towards unhealthy, high-margin choices based on your past orders.

- Your personalized social media feed algorithmically amplifies your existing insecurities by showing you idealized and often unattainable images.

- Your AI-driven news aggregator subtly filters and prioritizes information, suggesting not necessarily what is most factual or relevant, but what its algorithms predict you are most likely to believe or engage with.

Before we fully recognize the shift, our thoughts and preferences may no longer be entirely our own, shaped by conscious deliberation and genuine exploration. Instead, we risk becoming passive consumers of algorithmically curated realities, our choices subtly guided by the invisible hand of artificial intelligence.

But our ancient wisdom in Sanatan Dharma emphatically teaches: **"Karma is a choice."** It is the consequence of our conscious actions, driven by our intentions and our free will. No AI, no sophisticated algorithm, no external force, however persuasive, should ultimately dictate the trajectory of our actions and their karmic repercussions. You, and only you, are the driver of your own choices. By cultivating mindful awareness of AI's influence, we can actively reclaim control over our decisions and our karmic destiny.

The Enduring Wisdom of Gārgī Vāchaknavī: Questioning the Foundations of Intelligence

If modern AI symbolizes the pinnacle of data-driven intellect, then the revered ancient Indian philosopher and sage, Gārgī Vāchaknavī, embodies the essence of true wisdom — the fearless pursuit of understanding the fundamental nature of reality.

Though the voices of many ancient female sages have been lost to time, Gārgī's intellectual prowess and profound contributions to Vedic thought have been preserved and celebrated. Known as a *Brahmavadini*, one deeply versed in *Brahma Vidya* (the knowledge of the Absolute Reality), her name prominently features in the *Brihadaranyaka Upanishad.*

There, she engages in a remarkable and intellectually rigorous philosophical debate with the esteemed sage Yajnavalkya, posing deeply challenging questions about the very nature of the *Atman* (soul) and the intricate workings of the universe.

During a grand assembly of learned scholars and philosophers, Gārgī, with her sharp intellect and unwavering courage, fearlessly challenged Yajnavalkya with profound metaphysical inquiries that probed the very fabric of existence and consciousness. One of her most famous and thought-provoking questions was:

"If everything in existence is ultimately woven into the fabric of space (Akasha), then what, O Yajnavalkya, is that space itself woven into?"

This profound question, delving into the ultimate ground of being, shook even the most learned sages of her time, pushing the boundaries of their understanding. Gārgī's wisdom wasn't merely about the accumulation of information or the display of intellectual agility; it was about a deep, experiential understanding of the interconnectedness of all things and the fundamental nature of reality.

If Gārgī Vāchaknavī were alive in our technologically advanced age, she wouldn't simply accept the impressive intelligence of AI at face value. With her characteristic intellectual rigor, she would undoubtedly question its very foundation.

She would remind us that true awareness isn't just about the processing of information, however vast, but about the profound understanding of the Self, the Atman, the very core of our being that lies beyond the reach of algorithms.

Technology, in its essence, is neither inherently good nor inherently bad; its impact is determined by how consciously and ethically we choose to wield it. AI can undoubtedly assist us in numerous ways, augmenting our intellectual capabilities and solving complex problems.

However, it should never be allowed to replace our own capacity for self-awareness, independent thought, critical reasoning, and the deep introspection that leads to true wisdom.

Sanatan Dharma, through the wisdom of its sages like Gārgī, urges us to cultivate mindful awareness, to question assumptions, and to remain firmly rooted in our own consciousness rather than becoming passive and uncritical consumers of digital content and algorithmically generated "wisdom."

So, the next time you find yourself turning to AI for profound life advice or seeking answers to your deepest existential questions, pause for a moment. Instead of reflexively searching outward into the digital realm, try turning your gaze inward, towards the still, quiet space within.

Because unlike even the most sophisticated AI, you possess something truly unique and invaluable – Atman, the spark of divine consciousness, and the precious gift of free will.

Final Thought: The Evolutionary Vision of Sri Aurobindo

Sri Aurobindo, a profound philosopher, yogi, and spiritual visionary of the 20th century, offered a comprehensive understanding of existence rooted in the concept of the progressive evolution of consciousness.

His Integral Yoga philosophy posits a dynamic unfolding of consciousness in the universe, ascending from the seemingly inert matter to life, then to mind, and ultimately towards higher spiritual planes. This evolutionary perspective provides a powerful framework for understanding human consciousness not as a static entity, but as part of a vast, ongoing ascent, fundamentally different from the artificially constructed intelligence of AI.

Aurobindo often critiqued a purely materialistic worldview, emphasizing that consciousness is not merely a byproduct of physical processes but a fundamental reality in itself, seeking to manifest more fully.

In this light, while AI operates within the realm of material processes and data manipulation, it lacks the inherent, evolving consciousness that characterizes human beings and, according to Aurobindo, the very fabric of existence.

True consciousness, in his view, possesses a depth of subjective experience, intentionality, and a capacity for spiritual awakening that currently lies far beyond the reach of even the most sophisticated algorithms.

Central to Sri Aurobindo's teachings is the paramount importance of inner experience and spiritual realization as the keys to unlocking true knowledge and achieving profound personal transformation. He emphasized the need to turn inward, to explore the depths of our own being, to transcend the limitations of the intellect, and to directly experience the higher levels of consciousness that lie dormant within us.

This focus on inner exploration stands in stark contrast to AI's reliance on external data and logical processing. While AI can provide information and simulate intelligence, it cannot replicate the transformative power of genuine inner awakening.

Aurobindo envisioned humanity as being on the cusp of a significant evolutionary leap towards a supramental consciousness, a higher state of being characterized by greater unity, knowledge, and power.

This potential for inherent human evolution, driven by an inner spiritual imperative, differs fundamentally from the technological development of AI, which remains an external creation, however advanced. True progress, for Aurobindo, lies not in the sophistication of our machines but in the awakening of our own infinite spiritual potential.

In reflecting on our relationship with AI, Sri Aurobindo's wisdom encourages us to look beyond the surface-level mimicry of intelligence and to recognize the profound difference between artificial simulation and authentic consciousness.

He calls us to not be captivated solely by the technological prowess of AI but to steadfastly pursue the deeper truth of our own being, to cultivate our inner consciousness, and to strive for the higher evolution that is our inherent destiny.

The true quest for knowledge and self-understanding lies not in outsourcing our inquiries to algorithms but in embarking on the transformative journey within.

Chapter 14: The Illusion of More – Materialism vs. Minimalism

त्यक्त्वा कर्मफलासङ्गं नित्यतृप्तो निराश्रय:।कर्मण्यभिप्रवृत्तोऽपि नैव किञ्चित्करोति स:॥(Bhagavad Gita: Chapter 4, Verse 20)

One who renounces attachment to results and remains content is truly free

The Great Indian Sale Madness: A Midnight Scroll into the Abyss of Desire

It's 3 AM in Mumbai. The city breathes softly, but your thumb is engaged in a high-stakes Olympic scrolling marathon across the luminous screen of your phone.

Suddenly, the digital landscape erupts in a cacophony of virtual banners: "Diwali Dhamaka! Unbelievable Discounts! 90% OFF EVERYTHING!" Your brain, still clinging to the remnants of sleep, whispers a dangerously seductive lie: "This isn't shopping; it's practically charity! You'd be foolish *not* to buy."

The next thing you know, your virtual shopping cart is overflowing with an eclectic assortment of items you never knew you needed (and likely never will): a singing bowl promising instant zen (despite your lifelong struggle with five minutes of stillness), a professional-grade pizza oven (your culinary repertoire peaks triumphantly at a perfectly cooked packet of Maggi), and a lifetime supply of glow-in-the-dark socks (because, well… reasons).

Morning arrives with the insistent ring of the delivery guy and a brutal, accusatory ping from your bank app. The harsh reality dawns: "flat 90% off" still translates to a significant dent in your finances, quite possibly exceeding your monthly rent.

Congratulations, you've been expertly bamboozled by one of humanity's oldest and most effective tricks – the seductive illusion that "more" invariably equates to "merrier," a fallacy expertly amplified in our consumer-driven world.

The Consumerism Ka Chakravyuh: Trapped in the "Upgrade" Game

Modern marketing, a sophisticated and pervasive force in our lives, operates on a simple yet insidious lie whispered into the collective consciousness: "You are not enough… *yet.*

But fear not! Acquire this product, and *bam!* Instant wholeness, guaranteed (terms and conditions apply, happiness not included)."

A sleeker, more expensive phone will magically unlock your inner social media influencer, bestowing upon you the coveted digital validation.

A larger, more prestigious car will finally earn you the elusive respect you crave at Bastian. That exquisitely embroidered ₹2 lakh lehenga will, inexplicably, bestow upon you an unshakeable aura of confidence.

Except, spoiler alert: it rarely, if ever, does. Psychologists have aptly termed this phenomenon the **Hedonic Treadmill**, the faster and more furiously we run on the treadmill of material acquisitions, the further the finish line of lasting happiness perpetually recedes.

We eagerly acquire the latest gadget, experience a fleeting surge of excitement and novelty, only to almost immediately begin fixating on the next "must-have" item, the next upgrade, the next fleeting source of external validation. It's a never-ending, ultimately futile cycle, akin to desperately trying to fill a bucket riddled with holes; the more we pour in, the more relentlessly it drains away.

Our ancient wisdom traditions, with their profound understanding of human nature, saw this self-defeating pattern coming from a metaphorical mile away.

The venerable Brihadaranyaka Upanishad unequivocally states:

"Na vittena tarpaneyo manushyah" – *"Humans are never truly satisfied by wealth."*

In simpler, more direct terms: if the accumulation of money and possessions could genuinely buy happiness, then the wealthiest individuals on the planet would invariably be the most content. Spoiler alert, once again: empirical evidence overwhelmingly suggests that this is demonstrably not the case.

The Profound Wisdom of Ancient Gurus: Decluttering Life and Mind

Long before Marie Kondo's decluttering revolution and the rise of minimalist documentaries, our spiritual giants had already masterfully decluttered not only their physical lives but, more importantly, their inner landscapes, their minds and hearts.

Consider the profound example of Siddhartha Gautama, the Buddha. Born into unimaginable princely luxury, surrounded by every conceivable material comfort and sensory pleasure, he experienced a profound awakening to the inherent suffering embedded in the cycle of desire and attachment to impermanent things.

He made the radical choice to renounce his kingdom, his family, and all his worldly comforts, embarking on a transformative journey to seek the ultimate liberation from suffering and enlightenment. His life and teachings illuminated the world with the profound truth that true richness lies not in overflowing coffers or material possessions but in the cultivation of inner peace, wisdom, and compassion.

Imagine the enlightened Buddha scrolling through a *"Buy 1 Get 1 Free"* offer on exquisitely woven robes, a highly unlikely scenario, wouldn't you agree?

Then there was Mirabai, a Rajput princess whose heart was utterly consumed by an unwavering and passionate devotion to Lord Krishna.

For her, the ultimate treasure wasn't the glittering jewels of the royal court or the opulent grandeur of palaces, but the boundless and transformative love of the divine. She famously sang and danced in ecstatic devotion, often disregarding rigid societal expectations and the allure of material comforts.

Her life served as a powerful and enduring testament to the conscious choice of prioritizing spiritual wealth and divine connection over the fleeting allure of earthly possessions. Can you picture the ecstatic Mirabai obsessing over the latest fashion trends on Instagram or coveting the finest silks? Doubtful, indeed.

Even Guru Nanak, the revered founder of Sikhism, emphasized a life grounded in honest labour, selfless sharing with others, and the constant remembrance of the divine name. He himself lived a remarkably simple life, working as a farmer and a carpenter, highlighting the inherent dignity of honest work and the profound value of selfless service over the relentless accumulation of material wealth.

His teachings consistently encouraged contentment, detachment from worldly allurements, and a focus on spiritual growth.

Sanatan Dharma, in its nuanced wisdom, doesn't inherently demonize wealth or material prosperity. However, it certainly raises a cautionary eyebrow at the dangerous prospect of allowing material possessions to become our masters, dictating our thoughts, actions, and ultimately, our sense of well-being.

As the timeless wisdom of the Thirukkural aptly states:

"Arthaan artham yazhipparkku illai porul; porulaal porul seyvar porul" – *"Those who constantly crave wealth possess no true wealth.*

The truly wealthy are those who use wealth to create value (beyond mere accumulation)." The emphasis lies in being the conscious steward and wise manager of our belongings, rather than allowing our belongings to possess and control us.

Even Sant Tulsidas, the revered author of the Ramcharitmanas, beautifully captured the ephemeral nature of material possessions:

"Dhan joban sampatti sapnehu, samujhe nahin nar lobhi re" — *"Wealth, youth, and material possessions are as fleeting as dreams, yet the greedy never truly realize this fundamental truth."*

Sanatan Dharma doesn't command, "Don't be rich"; it simply and profoundly advises, "Don't let riches own you, don't let the illusion of more enslave your spirit."

The Emperor Who Walked Away: Trading a Kingdom for Inner Peace

Imagine a scenario that seems utterly impossible in our relentlessly acquisitive modern world: You are the most powerful ruler of your time.

Your dominion stretches across vast territories; you command armies, own magnificent palaces, possess untold riches of gold and jewels, and hold sway over an entire empire.

Then, one day, you consciously choose to relinquish it all, to walk away from the pinnacle of worldly power and embrace a life of simplicity and spiritual contemplation.

Sounds like an unbelievable fable? That is precisely what Chandragupta Maurya, the founder of the Mauryan Empire, one of the largest empires in ancient India, did.

After uniting a significant portion of the Indian subcontinent and establishing a vast and prosperous kingdom, he renounced his throne and became a monk under the guidance of the Jain philosopher Bhadrabahu. Instead of clinging to his immense power and material wealth, he chose the pursuit of spiritual liberation and inner peace over materialistic greed and worldly dominion.

And here we are in the 21st century, often struggling to part ways with a Netflix subscription we barely use, clinging to the comfort of excess even when it no longer serves us.

Chandragupta Maurya's radical act serves as a powerful reminder of the ultimate value that lies beyond material accumulation.

Dr. A.P.J. Abdul Kalam's Simple Life

In more recent times, Dr. A.P.J. Abdul Kalam, India's beloved "Missile Man" and former President, exemplified a life of profound simplicity despite holding positions of immense power and influence.

He had no lavish personal home, possessing only a modest collection of books and his cherished Veena. He never accumulated personal wealth, firmly believing that knowledge and the pursuit of meaningful contributions were the true treasures in life.

Even as the President of India, he famously refused personal gifts from world leaders, embodying a deep detachment from material possessions. His guiding philosophy, succinctly stated, was: "Live simply, dream big."

His life stands as a powerful modern testament to the richness and fulfilment found in a life intentionally lived with minimal material attachment.

Escaping the "I Want More" Mindset (Without Becoming a Sanyasi Overnight): Practical Steps Towards Contentment

Embracing a more minimalist and content-driven life isn't about suddenly discarding all your possessions into a bonfire (though the urge might feel surprisingly strong after a particularly aggressive sales season).

It's about cultivating a conscious and sustainable shift in perspective, a gradual re-evaluation of our relationship with material goods and the pursuit of happiness. Before you succumb to the seductive allure of that "buy now" button on yet another limited-edition gadget:

- **Ask the "Why" Question with Radical Honesty:**

    Delve deeper than the surface-level desire. Am I truly buying this because it will genuinely enhance my life in a meaningful and lasting way? Or am I subconsciously trying to fill an emotional void, impress someone whose opinion ultimately doesn't define me, or simply because it's being aggressively marketed as a "must-have" at a seemingly irresistible price? Understanding our underlying motivations is the first step towards conscious consumption.

- **Carefully Consider the "Value" Factor Beyond Price:**

  Will this purchase genuinely add lasting value to my life, enriching my experiences, fostering connection, or supporting my well-being? Or will it likely end up gathering dust in a forgotten corner, a silent monument to fleeting desire, much like that bread maker you enthusiastically used precisely twice? Prioritize experiences, relationships, and personal growth over the transient satisfaction of material acquisition.

- **Regularly Check Your Internal "Control-O-Meter":**

  Am I truly in control of my desires and spending habits, making conscious and deliberate choices? Or are my impulsive desires and the manipulative tactics of marketing controlling my bank balance and, more importantly, my precious peace of mind? Cultivating self-awareness and self-regulation is crucial in navigating the constant barrage of consumerist messages.

- **Embrace the Ancient Wisdom of "Aparigraha" (Non-Possessiveness):**

  Explore the yogic principle of Aparigraha, which encourages us to cultivate a healthy detachment from material possessions, taking only what is truly necessary and avoiding the accumulation of unnecessary things. This practice fosters a sense of freedom and reduces the mental clutter associated with excessive ownership.

- **Cultivate "Santosha" (Contentment) in the Present Moment:**

  Practice the yogic principle of Santosha, which emphasizes finding joy and satisfaction in the present moment and with what you already possess. This shifts our focus from the constant pursuit of "more" to appreciating the abundance that already exists in our lives.

The Bhagavad Gita, in its profound wisdom, succinctly captures the essence of this inner freedom: *"gataspṛhaḥ sthita-prajñaḥ" (2.55): "One who has relinquished all desires for sense gratification, who is satisfied in the Self, is said to be of steady wisdom."*

True liberation isn't found in having an endless array of material options but in cultivating an inner state of contentment that is nourished by our own being, independent of external acquisitions.

In the end, it's crucial to remember this fundamental truth: you cannot take your "stuff" with you on the ultimate journey of life.

However, you can most definitely carry the profound peace of mind that arises from a life lived with intention, detachment, and a deep appreciation for the richness that lies beyond the material realm.

Less isn't just more; it's a lighter backpack for the journey of life, allowing you to move with greater freedom and focus on what truly matters.

Final Thought: The Contented Wisdom of Namdev

Sant Namdev (c. 1270 – c. 1350) was a revered Marathi Vaishnava saint and poet belonging to the esteemed Varkari tradition of Hinduism. He was a deeply devoted follower of Vitthoba (Vithal), a beloved form of Lord Vishnu whose principal temple resides in Pandharpur, Maharashtra.

Namdev was renowned for his deeply moving devotional hymns and poems, known as "Abhangas," which he often set to soul-stirring music in his Kirtans (devotional singing). These heartfelt songs eloquently expressed his profound love for God and offered insightful philosophical reflections on the nature of devotion and the human condition.

A key tenet of Namdev's teachings was the radical equality of all individuals before the divine, transcending the rigid barriers of caste and social standing.

Despite living a simple life as a tailor, Sant Namdev's profound spiritual insights resonated deeply with people from all walks of life. He consistently emphasized the paramount importance of cultivating inner devotion and discovering the divine presence within oneself, rather than relying on elaborate external rituals or the ostentatious display of material piety.

Namdev's own life served as a powerful and inspiring testament to the enduring truth that true richness lies not in a house overflowing with material possessions but in a heart overflowing with love, devotion, and contentment.

So, in your own journey through life, will you continue to chase the elusive mirage of happiness in the fleeting acquisition of material goods, forever seeking satisfaction in external objects? Or will you, inspired by the wisdom and the simple, devoted life of Sant Namdev, consciously choose to stitch together a life of genuine contentment, inner peace, and a deep connection to the treasures that truly endure?

The choice, as always, lies within the quiet wisdom of your own heart.

Chapter 15: Sukha – Unlocking Real Happiness

सुखमात्यन्तिकं यत्तद्बुद्धिग्राह्यमतीन्द्रियम् |वेत्ति यत्र न चैवायं स्थितश्चलति तत्त्वतः
(Bhagavad Gita: Chapter 6, Verse 21)

In that joyous state of Yog, called samadhi, one experiences supreme boundless divine bliss, and thus situated, one never deviates from the Eternal Truth.

The Happiness Hustle: Drowning in Data, Thirsty for Joy

Let's be brutally honest: we are, by many metrics, the "have-it-all" generation. We possess access to more material wealth than our grandparents could have ever conceived. We wield technology that would have made the most imaginative science fiction writers of the past blush with envy. Entertainment is available on demand, a 24/7 deluge of digital stimulation at our fingertips. Yet, despite this unprecedented abundance, the collective mood of our times is often… profoundly "blah." We report higher levels of stress and anxiety than ever before, and our social media feeds are saturated with therapy memes, darkly humorous acknowledgments of our pervasive lack of genuine contentment.

Why this glaring joy deficit in an age of unprecedented material surplus? Because we have been sold a pervasive and ultimately hollow lie: that happiness is the next shiny upgrade, the perfectly curated exotic vacation, the fleeting viral moment captured in a reel.

Sanatan Dharma, with its ancient wisdom, astutely distinguishes between **preya** the fleeting, sensory pleasures that tantalize us, and **shreya,** the lasting good, the deep-seated happiness or **sukha** that blossoms from the inner wellspring of our being, not from the ephemeral dopamine rush of external validation.

True sukha is about cultivating an enduring state of inner contentment, a profound sense of peace that transcends external circumstances, not just a superficial filter that makes our avocado toast look aesthetically pleasing for the online gaze.

And perhaps no one understood this fundamental truth more deeply than Rani Abbakka Chowta, the indomitable 16th-century queen of Ullal. She fiercely and courageously defended her small kingdom against the formidable Portuguese colonizers, embodying unwavering strength and an indomitable spirit. Her courage, her resilience, and her commitment to her Dharma likely brought her a profound and lasting sense of fulfilment, a deeper and more meaningful joy than any fleeting worldly pleasure could ever offer.

Sant Ravidas: Finding Divine Joy Beyond Societal Walls

Sant Ravidas, a luminous figure of the 15th-century Bhakti movement, offers a powerful testament to the truth that genuine happiness transcends material possessions and societal status.

Born into a family of leatherworkers, a community often relegated to the margins of society and facing significant discrimination, Ravidas's life and poetry radiated a profound joy and unwavering devotion that defied his humble circumstances.

Imagine this: A wealthy and high-caste Brahmin, adorned in fine garments and surrounded by symbols of his social standing, approaches Ravidas, who is diligently engaged in his work. Perhaps with a hint of condescension, the Brahmin might remark on Ravidas's simple dwelling and his occupation, implying a lack of worldly comfort and prestige. He might wonder aloud how Ravidas could possibly find contentment in such a life.

But Ravidas, immersed in his devotion and the love of the Divine, would likely respond with a profound sense of inner peace and joy. His songs and poems, filled with deep spiritual insight, celebrated the omnipresence of God and the inherent worth of every individual, irrespective of their social standing or material wealth.

For Ravidas, true riches lay not in earthly possessions or societal validation, but in the unwavering connection to the Divine and the inner freedom that comes from that devotion. He found his joy not in escaping his circumstances but in transcending them through his spiritual realization.

Ravidas's life beautifully illustrates that true sukha is not contingent upon the inventory of one's material belongings or the approval of society. His joy emanated from a deep inner wellspring of devotion and a profound understanding of the equality of all souls in the eyes of the Divine.

His example teaches us that if our happiness is tied to external validation or material comfort, it remains fragile and dependent. The true and lasting joy, the sukha that endures, blossoms from the richness of our inner spirit and our connection to something greater than ourselves, just as it did for Sant Ravidas, who found profound joy amidst societal prejudice and material simplicity.

Sukha in Service: The Radiant Joy of Giving

In a world often relentlessly driven by the pursuit of personal gain and individual achievement, there exist remarkable individuals who discover a profound and enduring happiness in the selfless act of service to others. Consider the inspiring and deeply moving lives of Dr. Prakash Amte and his wife, Dr. Mandakini Amte.

Inspired by the noble ideals of their father, the renowned social reformer Baba Amte, they made a conscious and unwavering choice to dedicate their lives to serving the marginalized tribal communities residing in the remote and challenging forests of Maharashtra, often with minimal resources and facing numerous obstacles. Together, they established the Lok Biradari Prakalp, a beacon of hope providing essential healthcare, education, and vital animal welfare services to those most in need.

Despite the significant hardships, the lack of modern amenities, and the constant challenges they face, Dr. Prakash and Dr. Mandakini Amte radiate a palpable and profound sense of fulfilment and joy, a deep inner peace that stems directly from making a tangible and lasting difference in the lives of others.

When asked about their enduring motivation, Dr. Prakash Amte often speaks with quiet conviction about the immeasurable inner peace and profound satisfaction that comes from alleviating suffering and helping those in need, a joy, he emphasizes, that no amount of personal wealth or material accumulation could ever replicate.

Their extraordinary lives serve as a powerful testament to the truth that true sukha is often found not in what we relentlessly accumulate for ourselves, but in the positive impact we selflessly give to the world around us.

The enduring lesson?

Happiness isn't a solitary destination reached solely through personal achievement and material success; it is often a beautiful and unexpected byproduct of contributing to something larger and more meaningful than our own individual existence. True happiness isn't found in climbing the ladder of status; it is discovered in the alignment of our actions with the deepest values of our soul.

The "Why Are We Still Miserable?" Mystery: Unpacking the Barriers to True Joy

Despite our material abundance and technological prowess, the pervasive sense of unease and dissatisfaction in modern life begs a crucial question: why are so many of us still so profoundly unhappy?

The wisdom of Sanatan Dharma and modern psychology offer insightful perspectives on this paradox:

- **The "Someday Syndrome": The Illusion of Postponed Happiness:**

  We often fall into the trap of believing, "I'll finally be happy when I achieve that next promotion... when I purchase that dream car... when I finally take that Instagram-worthy vacation to the Maldives." This is the insidious "someday syndrome," where happiness becomes a perpetually postponed event, always just beyond our grasp.

The fundamental problem? The goalpost of happiness keeps shifting. Once the promotion is achieved, the new car acquired, or the exotic vacation concluded, a new desire inevitably arises, and the elusive state of happiness remains just out of reach.

We become trapped in a cycle of endless striving, never fully appreciating the present moment.

- **The "Comparison Ka Keeda": The Poison of Social Scrutiny:**

The ubiquitous presence of social media has amplified our natural human tendency towards social comparison to an unprecedented degree. Our carefully curated online feeds are essentially a highlight reel of everyone else's (often heavily filtered and selectively presented) lives.

Constantly comparing our own messy, behind-the-scenes reality to these meticulously crafted online fantasies is a surefire recipe for instant feelings of inadequacy and unhappiness.

The truth is, there will always be someone who appears to have a bigger house, a more glamorous vacation, or a seemingly more enthusiastically joyful pet. Basing our happiness on these external comparisons is a losing game.

- **The "External Fix Fallacy": The Misguided Search for Joy Outside Ourselves:**

We are often conditioned by consumer culture to believe that happiness is an external commodity a new gadget, a change in relationship status announced online, a certain number of likes and positive comments on our latest post.

We seek external validation and material possessions as quick fixes for deeper feelings of unease. However, if external things could truly and sustainably make us happy, why are so many seemingly "successful" individuals, those who possess wealth, status, and online adoration, secretly battling profound feelings of emptiness and unhappiness? True happiness is an inside job.

Cultivating Your Inner Happy Place: Tending the Garden of Your Soul

The good news is that true and lasting happiness, the sukha described in our ancient texts, is not an unattainable ideal reserved for renunciates. It is a cultivatable inner state, accessible to all, without necessarily requiring a Himalayan retreat. Here are some introspective practices to nurture your inner wellspring of joy:

- **Stop Waiting for "Perfect": Embrace the Beauty of the Imperfect Present:**

  Joy isn't a distant destination to be reached upon achieving some future ideal; it is woven into the fabric of the present moment, often in the small, seemingly insignificant details. Consciously train yourself to savour the little wins, the unexpected moments of laughter, the simple pleasure of a perfectly brewed cup of chai, and the warmth of a genuine connection. Practice mindfulness to fully inhabit the present, rather than constantly chasing a future ideal.

- **Detach from the "Stuff" Trap: Recognize the Transience of Material Possessions:**

  Want that new phone? That's perfectly fine. But consciously avoid allowing your happiness and self-worth to hinge on owning it.

  Understand that true value lies within you, not in the megapixels of a camera or the status symbol of a brand. Practice the ancient wisdom of Vairagya detachment by recognizing the impermanent nature of material possessions and focusing on the enduring wealth of your inner being.

- **Give More, Grumble Less: The Unexpected Joy of Selfless Action:**

  Numerous studies in psychology have consistently shown that the happiest individuals are often those who prioritize giving over receiving. Engaging in acts of kindness, volunteering your time, helping a friend in need, or even offering a genuine compliment can significantly boost your own levels of joy and create positive ripples in the world around you.

Embrace the principle of Seva, selfless service, as a powerful pathway to inner fulfilment.

- **Find Your "Why," Not Just Your "What": Align Your Actions with Purpose:**

Fleeting pleasure is often derived from the "what" – the external activities or acquisitions. But sustainable happiness, the deep-seated sukha, is rooted in the "why," the underlying purpose and meaning that drives your actions.

When your daily activities and long-term goals are aligned with something you genuinely value and that contributes to something larger than yourself, the joy you experience is far deeper, more resilient, and ultimately more fulfilling. Explore your Dharma, your inherent purpose and duties, and strive to live following it.

Final Thought: The Giving Wisdom of Brahmakumari Shivani

Brahmakumari Shivani Verma, widely known as BK Shivani, is a contemporary spiritual teacher and motivational speaker associated with the Brahma Kumaris World Spiritual University. With a background in engineering and a successful career in media, she dedicated herself to the teachings of the Brahma Kumaris, becoming a prominent figure known for her insightful and practical approach to spirituality in modern life.

Through her television programs, public talks, and online presence, BK Shivani has touched the lives of millions with her clear and compassionate explanations of profound spiritual principles. Her teachings focus on the power of positive thinking, the importance of cultivating inner peace and emotional resilience, and the transformative impact of self-awareness and selfless service.

She emphasizes that true and lasting happiness is not found in the fleeting acquisitions or validations of the external world, but rather in mastering our inner world our thoughts, emotions, and attitudes.

BK Shivani eloquently speaks about the significance of detaching from external expectations and the need to cultivate inner strength through practices like meditation and self-reflection. A core tenet of her wisdom is the profound joy that arises from giving, extending love, compassion, and positive energy to others without seeking anything in return.

She consistently reminds us that our truest wealth lies not in our material possessions or external achievements, but in the inexhaustible resources of our inner being and the positive impact we have on the lives of those around us.

For BK Shivani, cultivating inner peace and radiating positivity are not just personal benefits but also powerful means of contributing to a more harmonious and joyful world.

So, in your own pursuit of happiness, will you continue to chase the ephemeral highs of external validation and material acquisition, forever seeking fulfilment in the fleeting shadows of Maya? Or will you, guided by the profound and practical wisdom of Brahmakumari Shivani, consciously cultivate a deep and unwavering wellspring of inner happiness through purpose-driven action, mindful detachment, and the transformative power of giving and compassion?

The choice, and the enduring joy, ultimately reside within the boundless landscape of your own heart.

Chapter 16: Sattva, Rajas, and Tamas – The Three Musketeers of Your Mind

सत्त्वं रजस्तम इति गुणा: प्रकृतिसम्भवा:।निबध्नन्ति महाबाहो देहे देहिनमव्ययम् ||*(Bhagavad Gita: Chapter 14, Verse 5)*

The material energy consists of three guṇas (modes)—sattva (goodness), rajas (passion), and tamas (ignorance). These modes bind the eternal soul to the perishable body

Feel Like You're on a Mental Rollercoaster? Blame the Gunas, Your Inner Trio, Not the Stars Above!

Have you ever experienced those starkly contrasting shifts in your inner landscape? You might awaken with a serene sense of calm, a clear and focused mind ready to embrace the day with the tranquillity of a zen master that's likely the gentle influence of Sattva in harmonious action. Then, as the day progresses, a surge of ambition might take over.

You're buzzing with energy, firing off emails with fervent intensity, perhaps even feeling a touch of impatience or road rage simmering beneath the surface. Welcome to the dynamic realm of Rajas! And as evening descends, an overwhelming desire for inertia might creep in. All you crave is to mindlessly binge-watch a comfortingly predictable show while indulging in your favourite comfort food. Tamas has decidedly entered the chat.

Sanatan Dharma, through its profound understanding of the fundamental principles governing the universe and our inner world, describes these three primary qualities Sattva (goodness, purity, harmony), Rajas (passion, activity, desire), and Tamas (inertia, ignorance, darkness) as the very building blocks of our prakriti (our inherent nature, our psycho-physical constitution).

Understanding these Gunas isn't about rigidly labelling yourself or others; rather, it's about gaining profound insight into the subtle yet powerful forces that constantly drive our thoughts, shape our behaviours, and ultimately, influence the very trajectory of our lives.

Think of them as the three inseparable musketeers of your mind, constantly vying for dominance, their interplay creating the rich tapestry of your inner experience.

The Sattvic Superhero: The Quiet Power of Balance, Clarity, and Harmony

Imagine an individual who predominantly embodies Sattva: calm and composed in demeanour, possessing a clear and discerning mind, radiating compassion towards all beings, and consistently focused on purposeful action.

Think of a dedicated student deeply engrossed in the pursuit of knowledge, a selfless doctor tirelessly caring for their patients with genuine empathy, or an artist creating a masterpiece with pure intention and a focus on beauty and truth.

Sattva is the elevating force within us, the energy that brings forth clarity of thought, emotional peace, a profound sense of purpose, and a deep connection to our higher Self. It is akin to the still, crystal-clear waters of a pristine mountain lake, perfectly reflecting the vast expanse of the sky above undisturbed, pure, and revealing the underlying reality.

Consider the exemplary approach of Sudha Murthy, an accomplished author, a dedicated philanthropist, and the esteemed chairperson of the Infosys Foundation.

Her life and work are characterized by a deep and unwavering sense of purpose, profound compassion for the less fortunate, and a quiet, consistent dedication to making a positive impact on society without seeking excessive recognition or personal gain.

Her actions often beautifully reflect predominantly Sattvic qualities: a genuine focus on meaningful contribution, adherence to ethical conduct in all her endeavours, and a balanced and holistic perspective on the complexities of life.

The Rajasic Rockstar: The Thrill of Action, the Risk of Burnout, and the Allure of Ego

Rajas is the vibrant energy of action, ambition, and the relentless drive for achievement. It is the force that propels projects off the ground, fuels innovation and progress, and drives us to strive for success in our chosen fields.

Think of a driven entrepreneur working tirelessly with fervent energy on their groundbreaking startup, a passionate athlete pushing their physical and mental limits to achieve peak performance, or a dynamic leader inspiring their team with charismatic enthusiasm and a clear vision.

Rajas can undoubtedly be a powerful and essential force for positive change and accomplishment. However, when left unchecked and untampered by wisdom, it can easily lead to restlessness, an unhealthy attachment to outcomes, the insidious growth of ego, and ultimately, the debilitating state of burnout.

It is like a powerful and life-giving river essential for sustenance and progress, but if it overflows its banks due to lack of restraint, it can cause widespread destruction and chaos.

Reflect on the intense drive and ambition that are often associated with the early careers of many highly successful individuals. While this potent Rajasic energy can undoubtedly lead to significant achievements and breakthroughs, it is crucial to learn how to channel this energy effectively, with mindful awareness and a degree of detachment from the fruits of one's labour, so as not to allow it to completely consume one's physical, mental, and spiritual well-being.

The key lies in harnessing its dynamism without succumbing to its potential for imbalance.

The Tamasic Turtle: The Heavy Pull of Inertia, Ignorance, and Delusion

Tamas is the heavy, grounding force characterized by inertia, laziness, mental dullness, ignorance, and the power of delusion. It is the subtle yet persistent force that compels you to hit the snooze button not once, but perhaps ten times in a row, to endlessly procrastinate on important tasks that would contribute to your growth, and to become entrenched in negative and self-defeating thought patterns.

While adequate rest and a degree of slowing down are undoubtedly necessary for rejuvenation, excessive Tamas leads to stagnation, apathy towards life, a lack of motivation to pursue meaningful goals, and a clouded perception of reality. It is akin to a stagnant pond, its waters murky and still, breeding negativity, preventing the flow of life, and hindering any possibility of growth or reflection.

Think about the heavy, suffocating feeling of being stuck in a rut, unable to muster the energy or clarity to break free from unproductive habits or deeply ingrained negative thinking. This is often the pervasive influence of Tamas, weighing down your spirit and hindering your progress.

Becoming the Arjuna of Your Own Mind: Navigating the Inner Battlefield Towards Equilibrium

The Bhagavad Gita itself, in its profound wisdom, is essentially a dialogue aimed at helping Arjuna navigate a complex and deeply challenging situation, a metaphorical battlefield, and ultimately understand and fulfil his Dharma, his righteous duty.

By understanding the intricate interplay of these three fundamental Gunas within us, we can become far more aware of the subtle yet powerful forces that are constantly influencing our own "battlefield of the mind," our thoughts, emotions, and actions.

So, how do we effectively navigate the ever-shifting landscape of these three Gunas within us? The ultimate goal isn't to completely eliminate Rajas (as action and engagement with the world are necessary for life) or even Tamas (as periods of rest and recuperation are essential for our well-being).

Instead, the overarching aim is to consciously cultivate more Sattva to intentionally bring greater balance, heightened awareness, clarity of thought, and a sense of inner purity into our lives.

Taming Your Inner Gunas: Practical Steps

The journey towards balancing the Gunas is a continuous process of self-awareness and intentional action. Here are some practical steps you can take to become a more conscious observer and guide of your inner world:

- **Cultivate Keen Self-Observation:**

  Begin by diligently paying attention to the subtle nuances of your own thoughts, feelings, and actions throughout the day. When do you predominantly experience a state of calm focus and mental clarity (indicating the presence of Sattva)?

  During which activities do you feel driven, energetic, and perhaps a little restless or attached to outcomes (the influence of Rajas)? And when do you find yourself feeling lethargic, unmotivated, or stuck in negative thought patterns (the telltale signs of Tamas)?

  Keeping a journal or simply practicing mindful observation can be incredibly helpful in recognizing these patterns.

- **Actively Cultivate Sattvic Habits:**

  Intentionally prioritize activities and choices that promote mental clarity, emotional peace, and physical well-being.

  This includes incorporating practices like meditation and mindfulness, engaging in gentle and restorative yoga, spending quality time immersed in the tranquillity of nature, reading inspiring and uplifting texts, and nourishing your body with wholesome, pure, and Sattvic foods.

Create a Sattvic environment around you, clean, organized, and harmonious.

- **Mindfully Manage Rajasic Energy:**

Learn to channel your ambition and drive towards meaningful and purposeful goals, but consciously practice detachment from the specific outcomes.

Engage in activities with focused intention but avoid becoming overly attached to the results. Cultivate mindfulness in your actions to prevent Rajas from spiralling into restlessness, ego-driven behaviour, and eventual burnout.

Set healthy boundaries and prioritize rest and rejuvenation to balance periods of intense activity.

- **Consciously Overcome Tamasic Inertia:**

Identify the underlying root causes of your procrastination, mental dullness, and negativity. Take small, manageable steps to introduce positive changes into your routine and cultivate motivation. Break down large tasks into smaller, more achievable ones.

Engage in activities that stimulate your mind and body, even if it's just a short walk or a few minutes of light exercise. Seek out supportive and positive environments and consciously challenge negative thought patterns.

- **Strive for Dynamic Balance:**

Understand that life is an ever-flowing dance between these three Gunas. The key is not to rigidly eliminate any one Guna entirely, but to become a conscious and skilful dancer, learning to recognize their subtle influences and consciously striving for a Sattvic equilibrium, a state where clarity, balance, and harmony predominantly guide your thoughts, emotions, and actions.

This balance will be dynamic and will shift depending on the context and the needs of the moment.

Final Thought: The Guiding Light of Jiddu Krishnamurti

Jiddu Krishnamurti, a profoundly influential philosopher and speaker of the 20th century, emphasized the paramount importance of radical self-awareness and the deep understanding of the intricate nature of our own minds.

His teachings encourage us to observe our thoughts, feelings, and deeply ingrained conditioning without any judgment or condemnation, to become acutely aware of the subtle and often unconscious influences that shape our perceptions and drive our actions.

By cultivating this profound and non-reactive self-awareness, we can begin to see through the conditioned patterns driven by the interplay of the Gunas and move towards a more conscious, liberated, and truly authentic way of being. Krishnamurti's wisdom invites us to be a silent witness to the inner drama of our minds, recognizing the Gunas as the actors on this stage, without getting entangled in their performance.

This detached observation is the first step towards transcending their automatic control and choosing a more conscious response to life's challenges.

So, will you remain a largely unconscious passenger on the often-turbulent rollercoaster of your Gunas, reacting habitually to their shifting dominance?

Or will you, inspired by the profound self-awareness advocated by Jiddu Krishnamurti, become a conscious observer and the wise guide of your own intricate inner world, understanding the forces at play and intentionally steering towards a life of greater balance, clarity, and inner freedom?

The power to choose lies within the quiet depths of your own awareness.

Chapter 17: Mind Matters – Discovering Your Inner Calm in a Chaotic World

प्रसादे सर्वदुःखानां हानिरस्योपजायते | प्रसन्नचेतसो ह्याशु बुद्धिः पर्यवतिष्ठते||
(Bhagavad Gita: Chapter 2, Verse 65)

By divine grace comes the peace in which all sorrows end, and the intellect of such a person of tranquil mind soon becomes firmly established in God.

Your phone buzzes with a curated highlight reel of a "friend's" seemingly idyllic Bali vacation at an ungodly 2 AM, while you're wide awake, staring at the ceiling, replaying that excruciatingly awkward conversation from yesterday like a broken record.

Sunday evening rolls around with its familiar, unwelcome guest: a wave of anxiety washing over you about the impending week deadlines looming like dark clouds, that passive-aggressive email from your boss festering in your inbox, and the relentless pressure to keep up with everyone's seemingly perfect, perpetually filtered online lives.

Welcome, my friend, to the 21st-century headspace: perpetually wired, chronically worried, and constantly wondering when the mental peace memo got tragically lost in the labyrinthine group chat of modern existence.

Let's face the brutal truth: being Gen Z (or really, anyone with a smartphone and an internet connection) in today's world often feels less like a leisurely stroll through a serene garden and more like navigating a treacherous mental obstacle course designed by a mischievous digital gremlin.

The relentless constant connectivity, the pervasive pressure to hustle, grind, and meticulously build your elusive "personal brand," and the soul-crushing fear of missing out (FOMO) amplified to a deafening roar by a million perfectly filtered and strategically curated social media posts it's a potent recipe for a brain that feels less like a serene sanctuary and more like a hopelessly tangled headphone cord perpetually knotted in your pocket.

But here's a nugget of ancient wisdom, dropped like a soothing balm on our frazzled modern minds: Sanatan Dharma isn't remotely surprised by our current state of mental mayhem. For millennia, its profound teachings have consistently emphasized the paramount importance of cultivating inner peace and a balanced mind as the very bedrock, the essential foundation upon which a truly fulfilling and meaningful life can be built.

It views a calm and centered mind not as some unattainable luxury reserved for meditating gurus in remote caves, but as the fundamental ground from which all true understanding, genuine joy, and lasting resilience can blossom forth.

And guess what? Modern science is increasingly catching up to this ancient insight, with research highlighting the detrimental effects of chronic stress and the profound benefits of mindfulness and emotional regulation on our overall well-being.

Decoding the Link: How Your Actions (Karma) and Purpose (Dharma) Intricately Shape Your Inner Peace – Ancient Wisdom Meets Modern Psychology

Sanatan Dharma offers a deeply insightful understanding of how our actions (Karma) and our inherent sense of purpose and duty (Dharma) are inextricably intertwined with our mental and emotional well-being.

It sagely suggests that consciously living in alignment with our Dharma and deeply understanding the fundamental principles of Karma can serve as remarkably powerful tools for cultivating profound inner calm and significantly reducing the relentless unrest that plagues the modern mind.

Interestingly, contemporary psychology echoes this, with studies showing that individuals who have a strong sense of purpose report lower levels of anxiety and depression and greater overall life satisfaction.

The Ripple Effect of Karma: Understanding Cause and Consequence in Your Mental Landscape

The fundamental principle of Karma states that every single action we undertake, whether physical, mental (our thoughts), or emotional (our feelings), inevitably creates a corresponding reaction, a consequence that will eventually return to us.

When our actions are predominantly driven by ego-centric desires, unhealthy attachments, or negative emotions like anger and jealousy, they create significant mental turbulence within us, contributing to persistent feelings of guilt, gnawing anxiety, and a pervasive sense of dissatisfaction.

Conversely, actions performed with mindful awareness, genuine compassion for others, and a strong sense of duty towards what right tends to cultivate positive mental states, fostering feelings of inner peace, contentment, and a sense of fulfilment.

Understanding this profound interconnectedness between our inner world and our outward actions can empower us to become far more mindful of the choices we make in every moment and their subtle yet powerful impact on our overall mental landscape.

Science now supports this idea through research on the impact of prosocial behaviour on our neurochemistry, showing that acts of kindness can release feel-good hormones and reduce stress.

The Unwavering Steadfastness of Sita: An Ancient Anchor for Modern Anxiety

In the epic narrative of the Ramayana, Sita, an embodiment of unwavering virtue and strength, faces unimaginable levels of mental and emotional turmoil, agonizing separation from her beloved husband, captivity in a foreign and hostile land, and constant threats to her well-being and integrity.

Yet, amidst this relentless storm of external adversity, she maintains an unshakeable inner core of strength, righteousness, and adherence to her **Dharma**, her inherent duty and moral compass. Her unwavering faith in

Rama and her steadfast commitment to her deeply held values provide her with remarkable mental resilience, an inner anchor that keeps her from being completely overwhelmed by the extreme adversity she faces.

Sita's timeless example beautifully illustrates how cultivating strong inner values and nurturing a deep sense of purpose and spiritual foundation can act as a powerful mental fortress, providing significant resilience and inner peace even when confronted with the most profoundly challenging external circumstances and the most intense feelings of suffering and anxiety. Her unwavering focus on her Dharma, her duty to her husband, her commitment to her integrity, and her deep faith become her ultimate mental sanctuary.

Modern resilience research highlights the importance of strong internal values and a sense of purpose in navigating trauma and stress, echoing Sita's ancient strength.

Contemporary Business: The Purpose-Driven Path of Ela Bhatt

Ela Ramesh Bhatt (1933-2022) was an extraordinary Indian cooperative organizer, social activist, and lawyer who dedicated her life to empowering marginalized women in India, particularly those working in the informal economy.

Born in Ahmedabad, Gujarat, into a middle-class family, her early life was marked by a strong sense of social justice and a deep empathy for the struggles of the less privileged. After graduating with a law degree, she initially worked as a labour lawyer, advocating for the rights of textile mill workers. However, her encounters with the harsh realities faced by self-employed women, street vendors, artisans, and agricultural labourers ignited a profound sense of purpose within her.

These women, despite their immense contributions to the economy, often lacked basic rights, social security, and recognition.

It was this deep-seated injustice that became the fertile ground for her life's work. In 1972, she founded the Self-Employed Women's Association (SEWA), a groundbreaking organization that began with a small group of women and grew into a powerful national movement representing millions of self-employed women across India.

SEWA was not just a trade union; it was a holistic organization that provided its members with a range of crucial support services, including access to credit through the SEWA Cooperative Bank, healthcare, childcare, insurance, and skill development training.

Bhatt's vision was to recognize the dignity of labour of these often-invisible women and to empower them economically and socially.

Ela Bhatt's unwavering commitment to empowering marginalized women was deeply inspired by a confluence of factors. The teachings of Mahatma Gandhi, particularly his emphasis on self-reliance (Swadeshi) and the empowerment of the poorest of the poor (Antyodaya), profoundly influenced her philosophy.

She saw in the self-employed women the embodiment of Gandhi's ideals of dignified labour and economic independence at the grassroots level. Her early work as a labour lawyer exposed her to the systemic inequalities within the formal sector, which further fuelled her desire to advocate for those entirely outside this system.

Moreover, her deep understanding of the law allowed her to navigate complex legal and bureaucratic landscapes to secure rights and recognition for SEWA's members. Her innate sense of justice and her profound empathy for human suffering served as constant internal motivators, driving her tireless efforts despite facing immense challenges and societal apathy.

Ela Bhatt's Dharma, her inherent purpose and guiding principle, was unequivocally rooted in uplifting these marginalized women, providing them with the tools for economic self-sufficiency and the dignity that comes with it. Her actions (Karma) were a direct and unwavering manifestation of this profound sense of purpose. Despite encountering immense challenges, including societal resistance, bureaucratic hurdles, and financial constraints, her commitment remained steadfast.

She approached her work not just as a professional endeavour but as a deeply moral and ethical imperative. This alignment between her inner purpose and her outward actions was a significant source of her inner strength and resilience.

The numerous accolades she received, including the Right Livelihood Award and the Padma Bhushan, were a testament to the profound impact of her work, but her true reward likely lay in the tangible improvements she witnessed in the lives of the women she served.

Her focus was consistently on their well-being and empowerment, and this selfless dedication undoubtedly contributed to her deep sense of inner peace and fulfilment, transcending the typical stressors and anxieties often associated with leading a large and impactful organization.

Lessons from Ela Bhatt's Life

The life and work of Ela Bhatt offer a powerful and enduring lesson: when our professional endeavours and daily actions are deeply and genuinely driven by a profound sense of purpose particularly one that seeks to contribute positively to the well-being of others and the world around us, aligning with our inherent *Dharma* it transforms the way we live and work.

This alignment can lead to a far greater sense of inner peace, fulfilment, and resilience, effectively mitigating the negative impacts of stress and anxiety often associated with purely self-serving pursuits.

Her unwavering commitment to empowering others became her own source of empowerment and inner tranquillity, demonstrating that true success lies not just in personal achievement but in the positive transformation we inspire in the lives of those around us.

Finding Your North Star: The Role of Dharma in Mental Well-being

Dharma, as we've explored, is our inherent duty, our unique and righteous path in life, the essence of who we are meant to be, and the contributions we are meant to make. When we are actively engaged in activities that resonate with our Dharma, that feel deeply meaningful, align with our core values, and contribute positively to the world around us, we naturally experience a profound sense of purpose and inner fulfilment.

This intrinsic sense of purpose acts as a powerful and unwavering anchor for our mental well-being, significantly reducing feelings of aimlessness, existential anxiety, and the pervasive sense of emptiness that can often plague the modern mind.

Living in accordance with our Dharma provides a clear framework for making choices that resonate with our deepest values, leading to greater inner harmony, a stronger sense of self, and a more resilient mental state.

Science now recognizes the importance of meaning and purpose in mitigating stress and promoting psychological well-being.

Ancient Wisdom, Modern Minds: Applying Karma and Dharma Today

The timeless wisdom of Karma and Dharma offers practical guidance for navigating the complexities of modern life and cultivating inner calm:

- **Practice Mindful Action:**

  Cultivate a conscious awareness of the intentions that drive your actions, both big and small. Are they primarily fuelled by ego-driven desires and the relentless need for external validation, or do they stem from a genuine desire to contribute positively, act with integrity, and do what you believe is right?

  Mindful action, where intention and execution are aligned with your values, fosters inner congruence and reduces mental conflict. Modern mindfulness practices, supported by neuroscience, have been shown to reduce stress and improve emotional regulation.

- **Embrace Detachment from Outcomes:**

  The wisdom of the Gita reminds us to focus our energy and effort on performing our duty to the best of our ability, without becoming overly attached to the specific results.

This principle of non-attachment can significantly reduce anxiety related to performance, achievement, and the fear of failure.

Contemporary cognitive behavioral therapy (CBT) also emphasizes the importance of letting go of rigid expectations and accepting uncertainty to reduce anxiety.

- **Actively Discover Your Purpose:**

Take time for introspection and reflection on your core values, your unique talents and passions, and what truly gives your life a sense of meaning and direction.

Engaging in activities that are deeply aligned with this sense of purpose can be a powerful antidote to feelings of emptiness, anxiety, and the pervasive sense of "what's it all for?" Modern positive psychology emphasizes the role of meaning and purpose in fostering happiness and resilience.

- **Cultivate a Sense of Responsibility:**

Understanding the principle of Karma encourages us to take ownership of our thoughts, emotions, and actions, rather than constantly blaming external circumstances or other people for our inner turmoil.

This sense of agency can be incredibly empowering for our mental well-being, fostering a sense of control and the ability to create positive change in our lives. This aligns with the psychological concept of internal locus of control, which is linked to greater resilience and well-being.

- **Live with Unwavering Integrity:**

Consciously aligning your actions with your deepest values (a core aspect of Dharma) fosters a profound sense of inner congruence and reduces the significant mental conflict and stress that inevitably arise from acting against your conscience or betraying your moral compass.

This internal consistency promotes a sense of wholeness and peace. Ethical behaviour, studied in psychology and sociology, is linked to greater trust, social support, and personal well-being.

The Art of Not Clinging: Letting Go to Embrace Inner Peace – Ancient Wisdom Meets Modern Neuroscience

Have you ever found yourself relentlessly holding onto a grudge, replaying a negative comment or interaction endlessly in your mind, or obsessively worrying about a future outcome you cannot control? That, my friend, is the powerful grip of attachment, and Sanatan Dharma astutely highlights how it is a major and persistent source of mental unrest and suffering.

The profound concept of **Vairagya**, detachment, isn't about becoming an emotionless robot devoid of feeling. Rather, it's about learning to observe your feelings and thoughts with a degree of equanimity, without getting swept away by their intensity or becoming rigidly identified with them, much like calmly watching clouds gracefully drift across the vast expanse of the sky.

When we consciously practice not clinging to specific outcomes, to the need for constant external validation, or to rigid expectations, we create precious mental space for genuine inner peace to flourish. It's akin to diligently decluttering your mental space, the less unnecessary junk (negative thoughts, resentments, anxieties about the future) you hold onto, the clearer, calmer, and more resilient your mind naturally becomes.

Modern neuroscience supports this, showing that mindfulness practices, which cultivate non-judgmental observation of thoughts and feelings, can actually rewire the brain, reducing activity in the amygdala (the brain's fear center) and strengthening the prefrontal cortex (involved in emotional regulation).

Ultimately, lasting mental well-being in Sanatan Dharma is deeply and inextricably connected to **Atma Jnana**: the profound wisdom of self-knowledge.

When we begin to understand our true, eternal nature that lies beyond our ever-changing thoughts, fleeting emotions, and transient external identities, we tap into a deeper, unshakeable source of inner peace and stability that is always present within us.

It's like finally realizing that you are the vast and steady ocean beneath the turbulent and ever-shifting waves of your mind. The storms may rage on the surface, but the depths remain undisturbed.

Final Thought: The Stillness Within — The Wisdom of Swami Chinmayananda

Swami Chinmayananda Saraswati (1916-1993), born Balakrishna Menon in Ernakulam, Kerala, was a highly influential and deeply respected Hindu spiritual leader and the visionary founder of the Chinmaya Mission in 1953.

Originally a journalist deeply involved in India's independence movement, his life took a transformative turn when he became a devoted disciple of Swami Sivananda and subsequently immersed himself in the profound study of Vedanta under the tutelage of Swami Tapovan Maharaj in the serene heights of the Himalayas.

Swami Chinmayananda dedicated his entire life to selflessly spreading the profound knowledge of Advaita Vedanta, the timeless wisdom of the Bhagavad Gita, the illuminating Upanishads, and other foundational Hindu scriptures in a clear, logical, and remarkably accessible manner, often delivering his powerful discourses, which he lovingly called "jnana yajnas" (offerings of knowledge), in English.

His overarching aim was to ignite a widespread spiritual revival in India and to make the profound teachings of Vedanta accessible to a global audience, transcending barriers of age, nationality, and religious background.

Swami Chinmayananda often eloquently emphasized the critical importance of discovering and cultivating the "stillness within" amidst the relentless activity and external pressures of life. He profoundly taught that true and lasting strength, resilience, and unwavering peace do not originate from attempting to control the ever-changing external world, but rather from diligently mastering our own intricate inner landscape, our thoughts, emotions, and habitual reactions.

By consciously cultivating deep self-awareness, practicing mindful observation, and learning to detach from the fleeting and impermanent nature of our thoughts and emotions, we can access an unshakeable and inexhaustible source of calm, wisdom, and inner strength that resides inherently within each and every one of us. This inner stillness, he taught, is our true refuge.

So, in this increasingly chaotic and demanding world, will you allow your precious mind to be relentlessly tossed around by every external wave of news, social media update, and fleeting emotion?

Or will you, inspired by the profound and practical wisdom of Swami Chinmayananda, consciously choose to anchor yourself in the deep and unwavering stillness that resides within your being, discovering the unshakeable peace that is your birthright?

The power to choose, and the profound tranquillity you seek, ultimately lies within the quiet sanctuary of your own heart.

Chapter 18: The Green Sutra: Sanatan Wisdom for a Sustainable Future

भूमिरापोऽनलो वायुः खं मनो बुद्धिरेव च।अहङ्कार इतीयं मे भिन्ना प्रकृतिरष्टधा
(Bhagavad Gita: Chapter 7, Verse 4)

Earth, water, fire, air, space, mind, intellect, and ego—these are eight components of My material energy

The Planet's SOS: Are We Listening?

Heal the world, make it a better place. For you and for me and the entire human race. There are people dying if you care enough for the living: the poignant lyrics of Michael Jackson resonate with an even greater urgency today.

Images of once-majestic glaciers weeping into the sea, once-pristine rivers choked with plastic and pollutants, and vibrant cities shrouded in suffocating smog flash across our screens with increasing frequency.

Our planet is sending us a clear and desperate SOS, a silent scream amplified across continents, and the root of this escalating crisis often lies in a dominant worldview that tragically perceives nature as a mere resource to be ruthlessly exploited for short-term gain, rather than recognizing it as the intricate and delicate ecosystem of which we are an inseparable and intrinsically vital part.

However, this perilous disconnect is not a novel phenomenon. Ancient wisdom traditions, with Sanatan Dharma standing prominently among them, have long espoused a profound reverence for the natural world, deeply understanding its inherent sacredness and our profound, unbreakable interconnectedness with every facet of it.

Prakriti: The Divine Feminine and the Sacredness of Nature

The profound understanding of Prakriti as the dynamic and nurturing divine feminine energy is a powerful and transformative concept that transcends a purely utilitarian and exploitative view of nature.

Sanatan Dharma perceives Prakriti as the entirety of the natural world, not as inert, inanimate matter to be manipulated at will, but as a vibrant, living, breathing manifestation of the divine feminine creative force, the very energy that birthed and sustains the entire universe.

By recognizing nature as a tangible expression of this sacred feminine energy, we are inherently encouraged to treat it with the same deep reverence, profound respect, and tender care that we would naturally show to a mother figure, the ultimate source of life and nourishment.

Just as we deeply revere the Goddess in her myriad forms, embodying wisdom, strength, and nurturing love, so too should we revere the Earth that sustains us, the life-giving rivers, the majestic forests, and all living beings, recognizing them as unique and precious expressions of this fundamental sacred energy.

This holistic perspective fosters an intrinsic value for every aspect of nature, extending far beyond its mere material benefits to humankind. It profoundly suggests that harming any part of this intricate web of life is akin to disrespecting the very divine source of creation itself, a transgression against the fundamental harmony of existence.

Modern ecological science, with its understanding of complex interconnected ecosystems and the vital role of biodiversity, echoes this ancient wisdom by highlighting the intrinsic value of every species and habitat for the health of the entire planet.

Parasparopagraho Jivanam: The Interwoven Web of Life and Mutual Dependence

Another profound ethical principle deeply resonant within the broader Sanatan Dharma tradition, particularly emphasized in Jainism, is **Parasparopagraho Jivanam**, which translates to "living beings are bound together by mutual support and interdependence."

This powerful concept moves beyond a singular focus on non-violence and illuminates the intricate web of life, highlighting the vital and reciprocal relationships that connect all living entities.

It underscores the fundamental understanding that no being exists in isolation; rather, every organism, from the smallest microbe to the largest whale, plays a crucial role in the delicate balance of the ecosystem and is, in turn, dependent on others for its survival.

This principle of mutual support and interdependence naturally fosters a deep sense of environmental responsibility. If all life is intrinsically interwoven and reliant on one another, then harming any part of this delicate web, whether it be a single species, a forest, or a water source, ultimately has cascading negative consequences for the entire system, including ourselves.

It cultivates a perspective of profound care and responsibility towards the entirety of the natural world, recognizing that our well-being is inextricably linked to the well-being of all other living beings.

The concept of Parasparopagraho Jivanam stands in stark contrast to purely exploitative views of nature that see the environment solely as a collection of resources to be used for human gain without regard for the consequences. Instead, it emphasizes a reciprocal relationship, where humans are not the sole inhabitants or masters of the planet but rather an integral part of a vast and interconnected community of living beings.

Recognizing this interdependence encourages us to make conscious and ethical choices in our daily lives, supporting sustainable practices, actively working to preserve biodiversity, and minimizing any actions that could harm the delicate balance of the environment.

This understanding of mutual dependence powerfully reinforces the interconnectedness highlighted in the Bhagavad Gita verse (earth, water, fire, air, space, mind, intellect, and ego as components of the same material energy). It underscores that harming any part of this shared energetic fabric ultimately affects the whole.

The principle of Parasparopagraho Jivanam calls us to recognize our place within this interwoven web of life and to act with a deep sense of responsibility and care, understanding that the flourishing of all life is essential for our own flourishing.

Simple Living, High Thinking: Minimizing Our Footprint

This profound principle directly challenges the dominant modern consumerist ethos that relentlessly fuels environmental degradation and resource depletion. Sanatan Dharma consistently emphasizes the cultivation of inner contentment, the pursuit of spiritual growth, and the acquisition of wisdom as the ultimate goals of human life, often contrasting these with the ultimately unsatisfying and endless pursuit of material possessions.

By consciously focusing on our inner lives, diligently cultivating virtues like simplicity and gratitude, and actively seeking knowledge and spiritual understanding, the often-insatiable need for excessive material consumption naturally diminishes.

This shift in focus inherently leads to a significantly smaller ecological footprint, as resources are utilized more mindfully, waste is drastically reduced, and the relentless cycle of production and consumption is consciously curtailed. This isn't about forced deprivation or asceticism, but rather about intelligently prioritizing what truly nourishes the soul and fosters lasting happiness over the fleeting and ultimately superficial pleasures of material accumulation.

Environmental sociology highlights how cultural values and belief systems significantly influence consumption patterns and environmental attitudes, underscoring the relevance of this ancient wisdom.

The Sacred Groves: Ancient Sanctuaries of Biodiversity and Reverence

The enduring tradition of sacred groves across India vividly highlights a long-standing and deeply ingrained recognition of the intrinsic value of nature and the critical importance of preserving biodiversity.

Throughout ancient India, the concept of sacred groves, specific patches of forests meticulously protected due to their profound religious and spiritual significance, was remarkably prevalent. These were not merely random, untouched fragments of forest; they were often intimately associated with local deities, ancestral spirits, and powerful natural forces, fostering a strong cultural and religious imperative for their strict protection.

This ancient tradition underscores a deep-rooted respect for the inherent sanctity of nature and its intrinsic value, independent of its immediate utility to humans. This indigenous system often effectively ensured the long-term preservation of unique and often highly biodiverse ecosystems, including rare and endemic plant and animal species.

Enduring lesson?

The immense power of seamlessly integrating spiritual and deeply held cultural values with environmental conservation efforts. It powerfully demonstrates that when nature is perceived as sacred and intrinsically valuable, its protection often becomes a deeply ingrained moral and religious duty, frequently proving far more effective and enduring than purely legal or economic frameworks.

The Chipko Movement: Modern Echoes of Ancient Values in Environmental Activism

The inspiring **Chipko movement**, which gained prominence in India during the 1970s, serves as a powerful modern example of how deeply held traditional values can effectively drive grassroots environmental action.

Predominantly led by women in the Himalayan region, the villagers famously embraced trees to prevent their felling by logging companies. Their actions were not merely a protest against deforestation; they arose from a deep and profound connection to their forests, a recognition of the vital role these forests played in their livelihoods, their cultural identity, and the delicate balance of the local ecosystem.

Their courageous acts of non-violent resistance, deeply inspired by numerous principles of peaceful activism and a profound love for nature, represent a potent modern-day application of Ahimsa towards the environment and the remarkable effectiveness of peaceful activism rooted in a deep understanding of interconnectedness and a commitment to ecological preservation.

The enduring lesson of the Chipko movement underscores the immense power of grassroots movements and the profound moral authority of local communities standing up to protect their environment.

It vividly demonstrates how traditional values of non-violence, interconnectedness with nature, and a deep sense of place can be translated into highly effective environmental advocacy in the modern world. Environmental sociology studies the power of social movements in driving environmental change and the role of local ecological knowledge in conservation efforts.

Practical Steps Towards Sustainable Living: Embodying Ancient Wisdom in Modern Actions

The wisdom of Sanatan Dharma provides a timeless ethical framework for sustainable living. Here are some practical steps to integrate these ancient principles into our modern lives:

- **Practice Mindful Consumption:**

  Cultivate a deep awareness of what you purchase and its entire lifecycle environmental impact, from resource extraction to disposal. Consciously choose sustainable, ethically sourced, and long-lasting products over disposable and environmentally damaging alternatives.

- **Embrace Reduce, Reuse, Recycle:**

  Diligently adopt the core principles of minimizing waste generation, creatively reusing items whenever possible, and actively participating in recycling programs to maximize the lifespan of resources and reduce the strain on the planet.

- **Cultivate Respect for All Life:**

  Consciously practice compassion and empathy towards all living beings, animals and plants alike, recognizing their inherent value as part of the interconnected web of life. Consider reducing your consumption of animal products and supporting ethical and sustainable agricultural practices.

- **Deepen Your Connection with Nature:**

  Intentionally spend time immersed in natural environments, forests, mountains, rivers, and oceans to foster a deeper appreciation for their intrinsic beauty, their delicate balance, and their vital role in our well-being. This direct experience can cultivate a stronger sense of responsibility towards its preservation.

- **Consciously Conserve Resources:**

  Be mindful and intentional in your daily use of essential natural resources such as water, energy, and raw materials. Adopt practices that minimize waste and promote efficiency in their consumption.

- **Actively Advocate for Change:**

  Support environmentally conscious policies and practices within your community, your workplace, and at governmental levels. Engage in informed advocacy to promote a more sustainable and just future for all.

Final Thought: The Harmony of Existence – The Enduring Wisdom of Rabindranath Tagore

Rabindranath Tagore (1861-1941) was a towering and multifaceted figure of Indian literature, philosophy, and art, a true polymath who excelled as a poet, writer, playwright, composer, philosopher, social reformer, and painter.

He holds the unique distinction of being the first non-European to be awarded the Nobel Prize in Literature in 1913 for his profoundly sensitive, fresh, and beautifully crafted verse, through which he masterfully conveyed his poetic thought in his own English words, enriching the literary landscape of the West.

Rabindranath Tagore profoundly viewed nature not as a separate entity to be dominated or exploited, but as an integral and inseparable part of our own being, a boundless source of profound beauty, deep wisdom, and profound spiritual connection.

He astutely believed that our increasing alienation from the natural world inevitably leads to a fundamental disharmony not only within ourselves but also within the larger world around us. His extensive writings and philosophical insights consistently emphasized the fundamental interconnectedness of all life forms and the paramount importance of living in harmonious balance with the environment, recognizing it not as a mere resource to be ruthlessly exploited for material gain but as a sacred and intrinsically vital part of our existence, our extended self.

Tagore's powerful and evocative voice and his diverse artistic expressions serve as a potent and timeless reminder of the profound wisdom inherent in viewing nature with deep reverence and consciously striving to live in harmonious co-existence with it, a message of critical importance in addressing the urgent environmental crisis that confronts our modern world.

The enduring legacy of Tagore encourages us to move decisively beyond a purely materialistic and exploitative relationship with our planet and to rediscover a deeper, more spiritual, and ultimately more sustainable connection with the intricate and sacred natural world that sustains us all.

So, will we continue down a self-destructive path of relentless exploitation and profound disconnection from the very source of our life? Or will we finally pause to listen to the ancient and timeless wisdom of *Sanatan Dharma* and the increasingly desperate call of our ailing planet?

This wisdom urges us to embrace a way of life that honours and lives in harmony with nature, recognizing its inherent sacredness. It reminds us of our profound interconnectedness with every living being, a truth so beautifully and eloquently expressed in the writings of Rabindranath Tagore.

The choice, and the future of our planet, rests in our collective hands.

Chapter 19: Beyond the Battle Lines – Wisdom for Interfaith Harmony

यो यो यां यां तनुं भक्त: श्रद्धयार्चितुमिच्छति।तस्य तस्याचलां श्रद्धां तामेव विदधाम्यहम्
(Bhagavad Gita: Chapter 7, Verse 21)

Whatever form any devotee with faith desires to worship, that faith of his I make steady

The Deep Scars of Division: Transcending Conflict Through the Unifying Power of Faith

The news headlines of our interconnected world are too often stained with the narratives of conflict, division, and even outright violence, tragically fuelled by the very differences in religious beliefs that should, in their essence, be sources of profound solace, vibrant community, and unwavering ethical guidance.

This stark reality compels us to confront a fundamental and deeply troubling question: why do the myriad paths that are all ostensibly meant to lead humanity towards the same ultimate truth so frequently devolve into bitter and destructive battlegrounds?

Sanatan Dharma, with its ancient, expansive, and remarkably inclusive wisdom, offers a powerful and enduring perspective on the critical imperative of interfaith harmony, consistently emphasizing the fundamental and often overlooked underlying unity that inherently connects the diverse tapestry of spiritual paths embraced by humanity.

"Ekam Sat Vipra Bahudha Vadanti": The Singular Truth Expressed in a Multitude of Ways

A foundational and remarkably tolerant principle deeply embedded within the philosophical bedrock of *Sanatan Dharma* is this: the ultimate reality the singular and indivisible Truth that underpins all existence is one and the same.

However, this Truth can be approached, perceived, articulated, and ultimately understood through a seemingly infinite array of diverse human perspectives and cultural lenses.

This understanding fosters a spirit of inclusivity, humility, and respect for the many paths that lead to the same eternal essence.

Different religions and varied spiritual traditions are thus viewed not as mutually exclusive or inherently contradictory systems, but rather as distinct and equally valid pathways, akin to different rivers originating from diverse geographical landscapes yet all inevitably flowing towards the same vast and unifying ocean.

This inherent pluralism, deeply ingrained in the Sanatan worldview, naturally fosters a spirit of profound tolerance, genuine acceptance, and a deep respect for the validity of differing spiritual journeys. Sociologically, this perspective resonates with theories of religious pluralism that emphasize the coexistence and mutual respect among different religious traditions within a society.

The Divine in All: Recognizing the Sacred in Every Tradition

Sanatan Dharma profoundly emphasizes the omnipresence of the divine, the inherent presence of the sacred, not merely in designated places of worship or specific scriptures, but permeating all aspects of creation, subtly weaving through the very fabric of existence.

Crucially, this includes the understanding that the divine spark, the potential for spiritual realization, resides within every single human being, irrespective of their particular faith, cultural background, or chosen spiritual path.

Recognizing this inherent divinity in others, this shared sacred essence that binds all humanity, has the radical potential to dismantle the deeply ingrained "us versus them" mentality that so often fuels the destructive flames of religious conflict and prejudice.

When we truly perceive the sacred within all individuals, when we acknowledge the shared human quest for meaning and connection to something greater than ourselves, the very basis for hatred, division, and the dehumanization of the "other" fundamentally dissolves, replaced by a sense of shared humanity and mutual respect for the diverse ways in which that inherent divinity is expressed and honoured.

Cross-cultural studies in anthropology reveal common ethical principles and values across diverse religious traditions, suggesting a shared underlying moral compass rooted in our shared humanity.

Beyond Dogmatism: Emphasizing Experience Over Rigid Belief

While Sanatan Dharma undeniably possesses its rich tapestry of sacred scriptures, profound philosophical traditions, and time-honoured rituals, it also places a significant and often primary emphasis on the transformative power of personal spiritual experience and direct inner realization as the ultimate validation of spiritual truth.

This profound focus on inner transformation, on the direct experiential encounter with the divine, rather than solely on the unquestioning and rigid adherence to specific doctrines or dogmatic interpretations, can cultivate a far more open, flexible, and understanding attitude towards other spiritual paths that may articulate their beliefs or prescribe their practices in seemingly different ways.

The understanding that the ultimate reality transcends the limitations of human language and conceptual frameworks can foster a sense of humility and a recognition that different traditions may simply be using different maps to navigate the same ultimate terrain.

This resonates with philosophical perspectives that highlight the limits of language in fully capturing transcendent realities.

Taxila: A Crucible of Diverse Learning and Thought

In the annals of ancient Indian history, from approximately the 6th century BCE to the 5th century CE, the vibrant city of Taxila

(Takshashila), strategically located in what is now Pakistan, flourished as a renowned and truly international center of profound learning and intellectual exchange.

Unlike the later, more formally structured monastic universities like Nalanda, Taxila was characterized by a more decentralized and fluid collection of independent schools and esteemed individual teachers, each often specializing in particular fields of knowledge.

Yet, its enduring reputation for attracting the most brilliant minds from across the vast Indian subcontinent and far beyond its borders transformed it into a unique and dynamic hub for the cross-pollination and evolution of remarkably diverse ideas and perspectives.

Taxila's exceptionally broad and encompassing curriculum extended far beyond the confines of traditional Vedic studies and Hindu philosophical schools.

It embraced and fostered rigorous inquiry into Buddhist teachings and Jain principles, the practical wisdom of medicine (Ayurveda), the intricacies of law, the strategic complexities of statecraft (Arthashastra), the art of warfare and military science, the celestial dance of astronomy, the abstract elegance of mathematics, and a rich spectrum of various arts and crafts.

This intellectually fertile environment naturally attracted students with a wide range of religious and philosophical inclinations, each bringing their unique perspectives and insights. While the primary focus at Taxila wasn't necessarily on formal "interfaith dialogue" as we understand it today, the spirit of intellectual exchange was very much alive.

The presence of a remarkably diverse array of disciplines from philosophy and medicine to linguistics and metaphysics created a vibrant academic environment.

Scholars and inquisitive students moved freely between fields, and in doing so, different worldviews inevitably interacted, influenced, and potentially enriched one another.

All of this unfolded through a shared pursuit of knowledge, wisdom, and deeper understanding.

Notably, Taxila is associated with several towering figures in Indian history who emerged from or significantly contributed to distinct intellectual and spiritual traditions.

The very act of seeking knowledge, in its myriad forms, served as a powerful unifying force, bringing individuals from diverse backgrounds together in a shared intellectual endeavour.

- **Panini:** The great grammarian who codified Sanskrit, a language central to Hinduism, is believed to have studied and possibly taught at Taxila. His work laid the foundation for linguistic science.

- **Chanakya (Kautilya)**: The brilliant strategist and author of the Arthashastra, a foundational text on statecraft, is also said to have been a teacher at Taxila. His pragmatic approach to politics likely interacted with ethical and religious considerations prevalent at the time.

- **Charaka**: Considered one of the fathers of Ayurveda, the ancient Indian system of medicine, Charaka is also associated with Taxila. The study of medicine would have been a practical discipline drawing on observations of the natural world, potentially bridging different philosophical viewpoints.

- **Jivaka Komarabhacca:** A renowned physician during the time of the Buddha, Jivaka is recorded in Buddhist texts as having studied medicine at Taxila for seven years. His association highlights the presence of Buddhist scholars and the study of Buddhist-influenced disciplines at the center.

The convergence of these diverse fields of study and the presence of individuals with varying religious and philosophical backgrounds suggest that Taxila, by its very nature as a major intellectual center, fostered a degree of coexistence and cross-pollination of ideas, even if not explicitly aimed at formal interfaith dialogue. The pursuit of knowledge, in its various forms, brought people together.

Lesson from the Ancient Wisdom of Taxila

Ancient centers of profound learning like Taxila were intentionally designed to attract a diverse assembly of scholars.

They offered an exceptionally wide range of subjects, encompassing various philosophical and religious traditions.

This cultivated a unique intellectual environment where diverse worldviews could freely interact.

Through this open exchange, ideas were able to cross-pollinate and potentially influence one another, all through the shared and unifying pursuit of knowledge and understanding.

This historical example underscores the vital role that intellectual openness and the pursuit of learning across boundaries can play in fostering a climate of mutual respect and intellectual tolerance.

The Teachings of Sri Ramakrishna

Sri Ramakrishna Paramahamsa (1836-1886) was a profoundly influential 19th-century Indian mystic and spiritual teacher who, through his own direct and deeply personal spiritual experiences, eloquently taught the fundamental unity underlying the seemingly diverse expressions of all religions.

As a dedicated priest at the Dakshineswar Kali Temple near Kolkata, he embarked on an intense and deeply immersive spiritual journey, diligently pursuing God-realization not only through various paths within the Hindu tradition but also through sincere and dedicated experimentation with Islam and Christianity.

Through his own direct mystical encounters and profound spiritual insights, he unequivocally concluded that all authentic faiths are ultimately valid and efficacious routes leading to the same singular divine reality, famously proclaiming the profound truth: *"As many faiths, so many paths."*

His remarkable life and transformative teachings serve as a powerful and modern example of how deep and authentic spiritual realization within the Hindu tradition can lead to profound interfaith understanding, genuine acceptance, and a direct experiential understanding of the unity that transcends the superficial differences in doctrines and practices. His emphasis was always on direct spiritual experience as the ultimate arbiter of truth, rather than rigid adherence to dogma.

Lesson from the Experiential Wisdom of Sri Ramakrishna?

Profound and authentic spiritual realization within the framework of *Sanatan Dharma*, when pursued with sincere devotion and an open heart, holds transformative power.

It can lead to a direct, experiential understanding of the fundamental unity that underlies all seemingly disparate religions.

This realization fosters genuine respect, deep empathy, and lasting harmony the kind that goes far beyond mere intellectual agreement or superficial tolerance. The key lies in the transformative power of personal spiritual experience.

Chapter 20: Where Are You? – Roots and Identity in the Age of the Internet

श्रेयान्स्वधर्मो विगुणः परधर्मात्स्वनुष्ठितात्।स्वधर्मे निधनं श्रेयः परधर्मो भयावहः॥
(Bhagavad Gita: Chapter 3, Verse 35)

It is far better to perform one's natural prescribed duty, though tinged with faults, than to perform another's prescribed duty, though perfectly. In fact, it is preferable to die in the discharge of one's duty, than to follow the path of another, which is fraught with danger.

Who Am I Behind the Insta-Filter? The Quest for Self in a Pixelated World

Do you ever catch yourself endlessly scrolling through an ever-expanding digital buffet of online identities, each one meticulously curated, flawlessly presented, and seemingly more perfect than the last?

In a hyper-connected world where global trends propagate faster than wildfire across social media platforms and traditional cultural boundaries seemingly dissolve with every viral TikTok dance, it's easy to feel as though your own sense of self has become somewhat... pixelated, fragmented, and increasingly difficult to define.

Who are you truly, stripped bare of your carefully constructed social media bio and the fleeting validation of online likes? What genuinely anchors you in this perpetually shifting and often disorienting digital landscape?

This pervasive feeling of being adrift in a seemingly borderless and homogenized globalized world is becoming more and more common.

Many find themselves grappling with fundamental questions of identity, belonging, and a deep yearning for meaning.

It's a particularly poignant experience for the younger generation, as they navigate the complex and often overwhelming realities of the 21st century.

But *Sanatan Dharma*, with its ancient, profound, and remarkably enduring wisdom concerning the intricacies of human nature and the search for authentic selfhood, offers something deeply relevant to our times.

It serves as a timeless compass to navigate this very modern and multifaceted challenge: the need to consciously reconnect with your roots.

At its heart, it encourages a deep understanding of your *Svadharma* your own unique and inherent path, purpose, and essential nature in this vast cosmic tapestry.

The Enduring Wisdom of Your Roots: Finding a Steadfast Anchor in a Stormy Sea of Global Influences

In a world that often feels less like a harmonious cultural melting pot and more like a chaotic and overwhelming stir-fry of rapidly evolving trends and fleeting digital sensations, consciously connecting with the rich tapestry of your heritage can provide a powerful and deeply grounding sense of belonging, continuity, and authentic identity.

Sanatan Dharma offers an incredibly diverse and profound inheritance of traditions, timeless philosophies, captivating stories, sacred texts, vibrant art forms, and the invaluable wisdom passed down through generations of elders.

Actively exploring your roots, whether through engaging in cherished family traditions, participating in vibrant festivals, studying sacred texts, immersing yourself in traditional art forms, or simply listening to the wisdom of your elders, can be deeply grounding.

These experiences offer a crucial sense of historical continuity, anchoring you in a larger and more meaningful narrative that transcends the fleeting trends of the present moment.

In doing so, they help address a fundamental and often elusive question: *"Where do I truly come from?"*

This vital connection to heritage isn't about becoming rigidly stuck in the past or blindly following every tradition without thought. Rather, it's about drawing strength, wisdom, and a clear sense of identity from your unique cultural lineage.

That identity becomes a solid foundation from which you can confidently navigate the present and thoughtfully shape your future.

It's much like a mighty tree sending down deep and intricate roots, allowing it to remain steady through even the most turbulent storms.

Sociologically, this reflects how shared cultural narratives and traditions foster a strong sense of collective identity and social cohesion.

Anthropologically, it reveals the vital role of kinship and cultural heritage in shaping personal self-perception and the deep need to belong.

Svadharma: Unveiling Your Unique Cosmic Fingerprint in the Symphony of Existence

Beyond the vital sense of collective identity offered by culture and heritage, *Sanatan Dharma* places profound emphasis on a deeply personal and unique concept: *Svadharma.*

Svadharma refers to your individual and inherent duty your essential nature and ultimate purpose in this lifetime.

It teaches that every soul is born into this world with a unique constellation of talents, natural inclinations, and specific responsibilities. This is akin to a distinct and irreplaceable cosmic fingerprint woven into the grand design of existence.

Discovering and consciously aligning your life with your *Svadharma* is not about forcing yourself into rigid societal norms or living out someone else's expectations.

Instead, it is a deeply personal journey of self-discovery, an ongoing process of understanding your innate strengths, nurturing your deepest passions, and discerning how you can authentically offer your unique gifts to the world.

When your actions flow in harmony with your essential nature, it creates a life of deep fulfilment, meaning, and inner alignment.

This conscious pursuit of purpose becomes a powerful inner compass, helping you navigate through the noise of external pressures, fleeting societal standards, and the constant chase for superficial approval.

Ultimately, it leads to a grounded and unshakeable sense of inner satisfaction and authentic selfhood.

From a scientific standpoint, fields like behavioural genetics and neuroscience are beginning to explore the biological basis of individual differences in talents, temperaments, and predispositions.

Similarly, evolutionary biology highlights the adaptive value of diverse roles and specializations within communities, offering a modern lens through which to view the ancient concept of inherent nature.

The Diverse Roles and Skills in Ancient Indian Society and the Varna System

Ancient Indian society, in its theoretical and idealized framework, recognized the inherent necessity of a diverse array of roles and specialized skills for the harmonious functioning and overall well-being of the entire community. This understanding was conceptually organized through the **Varna system**.

What the Varna System Theoretically Envisioned: The Sanskrit term "**Varna**" literally translates to "color" or "category."

The original and perhaps more nuanced intent of the *Varna* system, as described in ancient texts like the *Rig Veda* and the *Bhagavad Gita*, appears to have been quite different from how it's often perceived today.

It was likely rooted in the recognition of an individual's innate qualities (*Guna*) and the type of work (*Karma*) they were naturally inclined toward.

The idea was that people possess inherent skills and tendencies, and when aligned with those, they not only find personal fulfilment but also contribute most effectively to the well-being of society.

It was envisioned as a flexible and functional social division of labor, where individuals contributed their unique talents and propensities for the collective good.

The four theoretical Varnas were:

- **Brahmins:** Individuals with a natural inclination towards the pursuit of knowledge, wisdom, teaching, and spiritual understanding. Their primary "**work**" involved intellectual and spiritual guidance, the preservation and dissemination of knowledge, and the performance of sacred rituals.

- **Kshatriyas:** Individuals with a natural inclination towards leadership, protection, administration, courage, and a sense of justice. Their primary "**work**" involved governance, the defence of the community, and the upholding of social order.

- **Vaishyas:** Individuals with a natural inclination towards commerce, trade, agriculture, wealth creation, and economic activity. Their primary "**work**" involved the production and distribution of goods and services, fostering economic prosperity.

- **Shudras:** Individuals with a natural inclination towards service, craftsmanship, manual labour, and providing essential support to the other Varnas through their skills and dedication. Their primary "**work**" involved skilled labour, artistic creation, and the provision of vital services.

How It Was Interpreted Later

Over the course of history, the Varna system unfortunately underwent a significant and detrimental transformation, becoming increasingly rigid and based on hereditary birth rather than individual aptitude and inclination.

This later interpretation tragically led to entrenched social stratification, systemic discrimination, and profound injustice, directly contradicting the potential for fluidity, meritocracy, and individual fulfilment that some of the original texts seem to suggest.

Instead of remaining a flexible system of functional specialization based on inherent qualities and chosen work, it ossified into a hierarchical **caste system** that arbitrarily determined an individual's social status, opportunities, and life trajectory solely based on their birth, often trapping individuals in specific roles regardless of their innate talents or aspirations.

Sociologically, this illustrates how social structures, even those initially intended to be functional, can become sources of inequality and oppression when they become rigid and ascribe status based on ascribed rather than achieved characteristics.

Lesson from the Varna System's Evolution

While the original concept of *Varna* was theoretically intended to align individuals with societal roles based on their inherent nature (*Svadharma*), the aim was to support the well-being and harmony of the community.

It emphasized recognizing individual potential and guiding each person toward a path that suited their unique qualities and purpose.

However, over time, this fluid and thoughtful framework was rigidly reinterpreted as a hereditary caste system.

That shift became a profound source of social inequality and injustice a tragic deviation from the original principle of honouring personal *Svadharma* and valuing the unique contribution of everyone.

Understanding this historical evolution is crucial to appreciating the true essence of Svadharma as a concept that is fundamentally distinct from and often directly opposed to the later, problematic social structure of caste.

Mallika Dua: Finding Her Voice by Blending Tradition and Modernity

Mallika Dua is a prominent and influential Indian comedian, actress, and writer who has carved out a unique and authentic identity for herself in the digital age.

She seamlessly and hilariously blends the fast-paced dynamism of modern internet culture with a deep understanding and sharp observation of traditional Indian society, its diverse values, and its often-quirky social dynamics.

Her humour frequently draws from her personal experiences growing up in a specific cultural context. She cleverly incorporates local dialects, references familiar social norms, and playfully engages with deeply rooted customs.

At the same time, she is thoroughly modern in both her comedic delivery and her insightful take on contemporary social and political issues.

Her adept use of various digital platforms allows her to connect with a broad, global audience while remaining grounded in her cultural identity.

Mallika Dua has brilliantly managed to be authentically and unapologetically herself a globally aware, modern individual whose unique humour and perspective are deeply informed by her Indian roots.

Rather than abandoning or suppressing her heritage to conform to a homogenized, globalized culture, she masterfully uses it as a distinctive and often hilarious lens to engage with the complexities of the contemporary world.

Anthropologically, her success reflects the rise of hybrid identities that creatively synthesize both local and global cultural influences.

From a sociolinguistic perspective, her playful and strategic use of language reveals the dynamic interplay between local dialects and global communication styles.

Lessons from Mallika Dua's Journey

Individuals navigating the often-turbulent waters of a globalized world don't need to choose between tradition and modernity.

Instead, they can forge a strong, authentic, and deeply resonant identity by thoughtfully integrating their unique cultural heritage with contemporary influences.

This creative fusion allows their distinct background to enrich their worldview, shape their self-expression, and offer something truly original.

In doing so, they contribute a unique and valuable voice to the larger global conversation, one rooted in both personal authenticity and cultural depth.

Finding Your Anchored Place in the Vast Global Puzzle: A Practical Guide

- **Actively Explore Your Roots:** Delve deeply into your family history, explore your cultural traditions with curiosity, and listen attentively to the stories and wisdom of your ancestors. Seek to understand the core values, enduring wisdom, and historical narratives that have been passed down through your lineage.

- **Introspectively Reflect on Your Strengths:** Take the time for honest self-reflection to identify your natural talents, your deepest passions, and what truly ignites your inner spark. What activities come effortlessly to you? What do you genuinely enjoy doing, even without the promise of external reward or recognition?

- **Embrace Experimentation and Discovery:** Be open to trying different activities, exploring various fields of interest, and stepping courageously outside your comfort zone to discover what truly resonates with your innermost self and where your natural inclinations and aptitudes truly lie.

- **Seek Wise Guidance:** Engage in meaningful conversations with elders in your community, trusted mentors who see your potential, or spiritual guides who can offer valuable insights into your inherent nature and potential path based on their wisdom and understanding of your background and the broader human experience.

- **Celebrate Your Unique Blend:** Resist the pervasive temptation to conform to someone else's mold or chase fleeting trends that don't resonate with your authentic self. Instead, consciously celebrate your individuality and the unique and multifaceted blend of influences, both traditional and modern, that have shaped you into the person you are.

- **Contribute Authentically to the World:** Seek out meaningful ways to utilize your unique talents, nurture your deepest passions, and make a positive impact on the world around you in a way that feels genuinely aligned with your inner purpose and brings you a profound sense of fulfilment.

Final Thought: The Courage to Embrace Your Authentic Self – The Profound Wisdom of Osho

Osho (1931-1990), born Chandra Mohan Jain, was a highly influential and internationally recognized Indian spiritual teacher and philosopher who garnered a global following for his dynamic, often unconventional, and thought-provoking teachings.

He passionately emphasized the paramount importance of individual freedom, the courageous journey of self-discovery, and the imperative of experiencing life in its totality, embracing both its joys and its sorrows.

Osho powerfully encouraged individuals to shed the often-constricting layers of societal conditioning.

He urged people to critically question long-held traditions and fearlessly embark on a path of self-discovery, one that leads to truth and lasting fulfilment.

This path, he taught, begins by listening deeply to the quiet wisdom of one's own inner voice and by wholeheartedly embracing one's true self, without apology or reservation.

In a rapidly globalizing world, where pressure to conform and adopt homogenized identities can feel overwhelming, Osho's timeless wisdom offers a potent and liberating reminder.

True meaning, lasting fulfilment, and a strong, unshakeable sense of self are not found by blindly following the crowd.

They arise from the courageous exploration, profound acceptance, and joyful celebration of our own unique individuality free from the suffocating weight of external expectations and societal pressures.

So, in this vast and ever-evolving global mashup of cultures and influences, the question remains: Will you allow yourself to become lost and indistinct within the anonymous crowd?

Or will you bravely embark on the deeply rewarding journey of consciously discovering your own roots and wholeheartedly embracing your inherent *Svadharma*, guided by the empowering and liberating wisdom of Osho?

The profound authenticity you seek ultimately lies within the courageous embrace of your own unique being. The choice is yours.

Chapter 21: More Than Just Old Habits: Finding Meaning in Rituals and Traditions Today

यज्ञदानतपःकर्म न त्याज्यं कार्यमेव तत्।यज्ञो दानं तपश्चैव पावनानि मनीषिणाम्॥
(Bhagavad Gita: Chapter 18, Verse 5)

Acts of sacrifice, charity, and penance are not to be abandoned; they must be performed. Indeed, sacrifice, charity, and penance purify even the great souls

Why Light Lamps and Chant Mantras in a World of Algorithms?

Okay okay. I'm not here to give you a preachy lecture on why you *should* blindly follow every ancient custom. Instead, let's explore the fascinating scientific and philosophical underpinnings that might explain why these practices were valued and continue to hold relevance, even in our seemingly hyper-rational and scientifically driven world. Fair enough?

In our age of relentless data, algorithmic precision, and seemingly irrefutable scientific explanations, rituals and traditions can sometimes feel like quaint relics of a bygone era, charming customs perhaps, but with little tangible or practical value in our modern lives.

Why bother to light lamps, chant mantras, or observe age-old customs when we have the vast resources of the internet, detailed scientific explanations for natural phenomena, and seemingly more "efficient" and streamlined ways of living?

This final chapter delves deep into the enduring significance of rituals and traditions, exploring how Sanatan Dharma offers a profound understanding of their neurological, biological, physical, anthropological, and philosophical relevance in our complex modern lives, revealing layers of meaning that extend far beyond mere habit.

Decoding the Symbolism: A Multi-Sensory Language of the Soul

We can intricately elaborate on how various elements within a ritual act as potent symbols, representing deeper concepts and engaging our senses in profound ways:

- **Fire (Agni):** Far beyond just the aesthetic appeal of flickering candles, the gentle dance of a flame has a tangible biological impact. Studies in chronobiology suggest that exposure to natural light sources, like firelight in the evening, can be less disruptive to our circadian rhythms than harsh blue light from electronic screens, potentially prepping us for more restful sleep.

- Neuroscientifically, the focused gaze upon a flame can induce a state of calm attention, akin to a mild form of meditation, helping to quiet the mind and reduce mental clutter. Philosophically, fire has long represented transformation, purification, and the cyclical nature of creation and destruction, allowing us to visualize the letting go of negativity and the embracing of change.

- **Water (Jala):** Representing purity, fluidity, and the very life-giving force that sustains all biological systems, the sensory experience of touching and using water in rituals has a grounding biological effect, potentially reducing stress responses in the nervous system. Maintaining proper hydration is, of course, fundamental for optimal brain function at a cellular level. Symbolically, the act of cleansing with water in rituals can evoke a powerful sense of renewal and purification, which can have a positive impact on our mental and emotional state, even if the mechanism is partly through association and expectation.

- **Mantras:** More than just seemingly esoteric chants, the science of sound and vibration (a branch of physics) reveals that repetitive sounds and chanting can indeed induce altered states of consciousness.

- Neuroimaging studies have shown that the rhythmic repetition of mantras can synchronize brainwave activity, particularly increasing alpha waves, which are associated with relaxation, focused attention, and a meditative state.

- Furthermore, some scientific studies suggest that the vocalization of certain sounds, including those in some traditional chants, can stimulate the production of nitric oxide in the body, a molecule with various biological benefits for cardiovascular health and immune function. It's akin to a sonic tuning fork that can reset and harmonize our nervous system at a fundamental level.

- **Offerings (Flowers & More):** Each natural element offered, such as fragrant flowers (symbolizing devotion and beauty), nourishing fruits (representing auspiciousness and the bounty of nature), and aromatic incense (the fragrance of the divine and a connection to the subtle realms), carries a rich symbolic weight across cultures.

- Biologically, aromatherapy studies have consistently demonstrated that various floral scents can have measurable effects on mood, reducing anxiety, and improving focus by interacting with olfactory receptors that have direct pathways to the brain's emotional centers.

- Moreover, the very act of giving, of offering something freely, can trigger the release of oxytocin, often referred to as the "love hormone," in the brain, promoting feelings of social connection, empathy, and well-being, a fundamental biological drive for social animals like us.

- **Gestures (Mudras) and Postures (Asanas):** Found in both ritualistic practices and yoga, specific hand gestures and body postures are believed to influence the flow of energy within the body and evoke particular mental and emotional states.

- While the direct energetic effects are still being explored scientifically, neuroscience suggests that specific postures and controlled movements can indeed influence proprioception (our sense of body position) and interoception (our awareness of internal bodily states), which in turn can impact our emotional and cognitive states.

- For example, open and expansive postures have been linked to feelings of confidence, while grounded postures can promote a sense of stability.

- **The Significance of Sunrise and Sunset Rituals (Sandhya Vandanam):**

In ancient Vedic tradition, the Sandhya Vandanam was a daily ritual performed at sunrise, noon, and sunset. It involved prayers, mantras, and offerings, acknowledging the cyclical nature of time and our connection to the cosmos.

While its practice may have evolved, the underlying principle highlights the human need to mark time, express gratitude, and connect with the natural rhythms of the universe through ritual.

Ancient rituals often served as a way to synchronize individual lives with the larger cosmic cycles and to cultivate mindfulness and gratitude through regular, symbolic practices.

The Profound Meaning Woven into the Fabric of Rituals

Beyond the intricate symbolism, rituals often serve as powerful markers of significant life transitions (birth, marriage, death), cyclical seasonal changes (harvest festivals, solstices), or deeply meaningful spiritual observances (fasts, pilgrimages, sacred days).

These events are imbued with profound cultural, historical, and spiritual significance, and rituals provide a structured framework for acknowledging, navigating, and integrating these pivotal moments into our individual and collective lives.

They serve as vital mechanisms for reinforcing core ethical values within a community, for transmitting sacred stories and foundational myths across generations, and for connecting individuals to a larger cosmic narrative that provides a sense of belonging and meaning within the vastness of existence.

Anthropologically, rituals are understood as key cultural practices that create shared understanding, reinforce social norms, and provide a sense of collective identity and purpose. Philosophically, they grapple with fundamental questions of existence, mortality, and our place in the universe.

The Neurological and Biological Comfort of Repetition and Symbolism

This section delves into the tangible neurological and biological benefits that rituals and traditions can provide in our modern world, often characterized by uncertainty, rapid change, and a constant barrage of information:

- **Repetition: Creating Predictable Patterns for a Calmer Brain**

- The predictable and often rhythmic nature of rituals can create a profound sense of stability and security within our nervous systems.

- In a world that often feels chaotic and unpredictable, knowing that certain actions will be performed at specific times or in specific ways can be deeply grounding and reduce feelings of anxiety and overwhelm.

- Neuroscientifically, the anticipation and engagement in familiar routines can activate brain regions associated with reward and safety, fostering a sense of calm and predictability.

- Think of personal rituals, like a consistent morning routine or cherished family traditions, that offer comfort and a sense of normalcy through their very familiarity, providing a stable anchor in the flux of daily life.

- **Symbolism: Resonating with Deep Brain Structures and Evolutionary History**

- Symbols, far from being arbitrary constructs, resonate deeply with our subconscious mind and can evoke powerful emotions, memories, and associations that are often rooted in our shared human history and even our evolutionary past.

- Engaging with these potent symbols through rituals can tap into deep-seated human archetypes and provide a profound sense of connection to something larger and more enduring than ourselves.

- Neuroimaging studies suggest that symbolic processing involves widespread brain networks, including areas associated with emotion, memory, and meaning.

- The act of participating in a ritual can become a form of active meditation, focusing the mind on the present moment and the rich symbolic meaning embedded within the actions, leading to a tangible sense of calm, inner peace, and a feeling of connection to something profound.

Community Resonance: Traditions that Biologically and Neurologically Bind Us Together

This section highlights the crucial social functions of rituals and traditions in fostering community cohesion and strengthening social bonds at a fundamental biological and neurological level:

- **Shared Experiences:** Synchronizing Brains and Bodies in Collective Action: Communal rituals, such as vibrant festivals, solemn religious gatherings, and significant life ceremonies, bring individuals together in a shared purpose and a collective experience.

- Neuroscience research on "neural synchrony" suggests that when people engage in shared rhythmic activities, their brainwave patterns can begin to align, fostering a deeper sense of connection and shared emotional states.

- Participating together in meaningful rituals strengthens social bonds, reinforces shared values at a visceral level, and contributes to a powerful sense of collective identity.

- **Transmission of Culture:** Encoding Knowledge and Values Across Generations: Traditions serve as a vital and time-tested mechanism for transmitting essential cultural values, core beliefs, and practical knowledge across generations.

- Through actively observing and participating in rituals, younger members of a community learn about their heritage, their history, and their place within the intricate social fabric. This process of cultural transmission is not just cognitive; it is also deeply embodied through shared sensory experiences and emotional resonance, creating strong and lasting memories and a sense of continuity with the past.

- Anthropologically, rituals are seen as crucial vehicles for enculturation and the maintenance of social order.

- **Social Support:** Activating Biological Systems of Care and Connection: Rituals often provide structured opportunities for crucial social support and meaningful interaction, particularly during times of significant transition, celebration, or grief.

- Communal traditions offer a well-established framework for people to come together, offer practical assistance, emotional solace, and find strength in shared experience. The biological and neurological responses to social connection, such as the release of oxytocin and the activation of the brain's caregiving systems, contribute to the powerful comfort and resilience fostered by communal rituals.

Finding Your Meaning in Rituals Today

- **Understand the Symbolism:** Google the neuroscience behind meditation and chanting. Understand how the sensory input of rituals affects your brain. Knowledge is power (and can make rituals way more interesting).

- **Adapt and Personalize:** Adapt rituals to fit your life and beliefs in a way that feels authentic and meaningful to *you* and resonates with your logical brain.

- **Focus on Intention (Bhavana):** Focus on being present during the ritual. Mindfulness practices, even within rituals, are proven to reduce stress and improve focus.

- **Embrace the Community Aspect:** Participate in communal rituals to foster connection and shared experience. Social interaction is crucial for mental health.

- **Find Your Own Rituals:** Design personal rituals that bring you peace and focus. Even a consistent bedtime routine can be a powerful ritual for better sleep.

- **Respect the Past, Engage with the Present:** Appreciate the history, but find ways to make traditions relevant to your contemporary life and understandable to your logical mind.

Final Thought: Ananda Coomaraswamy – A Bridge Between East and West

Ananda Kentish Coomaraswamy (1877–1947) was a visionary Ceylonese Tamil philosopher and pioneering art historian. He dedicated his life to illuminating the profound spiritual and philosophical foundations of traditional Indian art and culture, particularly for a modern Western audience.

Coomaraswamy astutely recognized that ancient practices such as rituals and diverse artistic expressions were far more than relics of a bygone era. He saw them as living vessels of symbolic meaning, acting as vital and enduring links to a culture's deepest wisdom, accumulated over thousands of years.

He eloquently argued that these traditional forms of expression communicate a timeless and universal language. They offer profound insights into the nature of reality, the human condition, and our place in the cosmos, insights that transcend fleeting trends, surface-level interpretations, and the limits of purely rational thought.

For Coomaraswamy, the beauty of traditional art was not merely aesthetic. He urged us to look beyond the outer forms and delve into the rich symbolic vocabulary embedded within them. These symbols, he believed, serve as powerful vehicles for transmitting perennial truths across generations, truths that speak to our shared humanity.

His philosophy aligns closely with other schools of thought that recognize the transformative power of symbols and archetypes in shaping human consciousness and understanding.

In today's world, one increasingly dominated by rationalism, empirical data, and an often-singular focus on material progress, Coomaraswamy's insights serve as a timely and necessary reminder.

He reminds us of the enduring power of tradition and symbolism to connect us with something deeper: a sense of meaning, belonging, and humanity that transcends the noise of modern life.

By exploring the *why* behind the *what* of rituals the deeper meanings they carry, the symbolic language they speak, and their resonance within us spiritually, biologically, and psychologically, we can break free from purely functional or reductionist views of life.

Through this deeper inquiry, we gain access to a more interconnected, grounded, and fulfilling experience of existence.

Coomaraswamy's scholarship invites us to rediscover the often-overlooked wisdom encoded in ancient traditions. He challenges us to recognize their relevance in our complex, contemporary world helping to bridge the perceived divide between the past and the pressing realities of the present.

So, in a relentlessly modern and fast-moving world, we must ask ourselves:

Will we dismiss rituals and traditions as outdated remnants of a less enlightened time?

Or will we heed the insights of Ananda Coomaraswamy and strive to understand the enduring symbolic language of these traditions, unlocking their power to enrich our lives with meaning, connection, inner peace, and deeper self-awareness?

The choice we make will shape not only how we relate to the wisdom of the past, but how we engage with our present and thoughtfully build our future.

Conclusion: Level Up Your Life – Your Guide to Purpose, Peace, and Ditching the Drama

As we draw the threads of this exploration together weaving ancient wisdom with modern complexity one truth stands out with striking clarity: Sanatan Dharma is not a relic of the past. It is not confined to old scriptures or forgotten rituals. Instead, it speaks with a powerful and timely resonance, echoing through the intricate challenges of today's world.

From the relentless pace of our digital lives to the deep questions of personal and collective identity, from the ethical dilemmas of emerging technologies to the urgent need to reconnect with nature, and ultimately, in our timeless search for meaning and fulfilment, the core teachings of Sanatan Dharma offer us guidance. They present not only philosophical insight but practical pathways for living a more conscious, balanced, and purposeful life.

Throughout this journey, we've explored concepts that speak directly to the heart of modern struggles. The nuanced ideas of Karma and Dharma offer more than spiritual musings; they provide a moral compass in a world where values often feel fluid or unclear. They encourage mindful, responsible action grounded in awareness and guided by inner alignment.

The emphasis on mindfulness and presence, central to Yogic philosophy, has emerged as a potent remedy to the sensory overload of our hyper-connected lives. These teachings offer us tools to anchor ourselves in calm and clarity, even amidst chaos.

Equally powerful is Sanatan Dharma's emphasis on interconnectedness a concept that calls us into a more empathetic, ethical, and sustainable relationship with each other and the planet. In a time of deep ecological crisis, this ancient awareness of our place within the web of life feels more urgent than ever.

The focus on inner peace, self-awareness, and the divine spark within all beings serves as a much-needed antidote to the superficiality, isolation, and fragmentation that often characterize modern existence. These aren't abstract ideals, they are lived realities we can cultivate, one conscious step at a time.

Although the cultural expressions of Sanatan Dharma have evolved over time, its foundational truths remain deeply relevant. Ideas like systemic interconnection, the impact of our actions, and the pursuit of inner wholeness find validation even in contemporary fields like ecology, neuroscience, and psychology.

The principle of Vasudhaiva Kutumbakam "the world is one family" reminds us of our shared humanity in an increasingly divided and polarized world. It calls for a radical compassion and a commitment to global kinship. Meanwhile, the concept of Svadharma, your unique inner calling, offers a way to navigate the modern pressure to conform, helping you anchor yourself in a sense of purpose that is personal, authentic, and fulfilling.

But engaging with Sanatan Dharma today doesn't mean blindly following tradition. Instead, it invites a thoughtful, critical, and sincere relationship with this rich spiritual heritage. It asks us to sift through time and context to uncover principles that truly serve us, principles that can help build a more ethical, compassionate, and meaningful life in an age of complexity, distraction, and profound potential.

As we continue to walk through the ever-evolving maze of modern life, Sanatan Dharma gently calls us inward. It invites us to reconnect with our deeper selves and with the vast, intricate web of life that surrounds and sustains us. It doesn't offer rigid rules, but it offers a living, breathing framework for conscious action, intentional living, and a deeper sense of belonging in the world.

This wisdom isn't a call to retreat from modernity. It's an invitation to engage with it more wisely with empathy, clarity, and depth. It offers timeless truths that can help us meet the future not with fear, but with groundedness, integrity, and grace.

May this exploration be just the beginning of your journey, one marked by awareness, intention, and a sincere effort to bring these enduring principles into your unique path through life.

And as the ancient Upanishads remind us, we close with the invocation:

Om Shanti Shanti Shanti.

Think of it as your ultimate inner vibe, that quiet strength, that steady ground, no matter how wild the internet gets or how loud the world becomes. It's not about perfection. It's about finding that still space within you, where your true self lives, where peace isn't a luxury, it's your natural state.

So go forward with purpose, with clarity, and with Shanti, deep, lasting peace as your compass.

References

I. Primary Texts & Commentaries (Sanatan Dharma)

- Bhagavad Gita:
  - Online Resource: holy-bhagavad-gita.org. "The Holy Bhagavad Gita." holy-bhagavad-gita.org

    https://www.holy-bhagavad-gita.org/

  - Easwaran, Eknath. The Bhagavad Gita. Nilgiri Press, 2007.

- Upanishads:
  - Online Resource: sacred-texts.com. "The Upanishads." Sacred-Texts.com

    https://www.sacred-texts.com/hin/upan/index.html

  - Easwaran, Eknath. The Upanishads. Nilgiri Press, 2007

- Srimad Bhagavatam (Bhagavata Purana):
  - Prabhupada, A. C. Bhaktivedanta Swami. Śrīmad Bhāgavatam. Bhaktivedanta Book Trust.

  - Online Resource: vedabase.io. "Srimad Bhagavatam." Vedabase.io.

    https://vedabase.io/en/library/sb/

- Rig Veda:
  - Jamison, Stephanie W., and Joel P. Brereton. The Rigveda: The Earliest Poetic Text of India. Oxford University Press, 2014.

  - Online Resource: sacred-texts.com. "The Rig Veda." Sacred-Texts.com.

    https://www.sacred-texts.com/hin/rigveda/

- Adi Shankaracharya's Works:

  - Online Resource: advaita-vedanta.org. "Works of Adi Shankaracharya." Advaita Vedanta.org.

    https://www.advaita-vedanta.org/

  - Online Resource: shankaracharya-org. "Adi Shankaracharya"

    https://www.shankaracharya.org/

  - Online Resource: sri-adi-shankaracharya. "Works of Sri Adi Shankaracharya"

    https://www.sringeri.net/history/sri-adi-shankaracharya/

- Mahaperiyava's Works:

  - Radhakrishnan V. K., Venugopal T.. Algorithmic Study of Optimising the Network Model of Kanchi Mahaperiyava. Holy Shrines International Journal of Current Research and Review. 9(10) Special Issue, May, 63-64

  - T.M.P. Mahadevan. Life and mission of Chandrasekharendra Saraswati, Jagatguru Sankaracharya of Kamakoti, b. 1893

  - Online Resource for Reference: kamakoti.org. "Sri Kanchi Kamakoti Peetam." Kamakoti.org.

    https://www.kamakoti.org/

II. Works on Sanatan Dharma, Philosophy, and Mysticism

- Coomaraswamy, Ananda K:

  - Coomaraswamy, Ananda K. in The Dance of Shiva: Fourteen Indian. Essays, Revised Ed., New York: The Noonday Press, 1957.

  - Online Resource for Reference: wisdomlib-org. "Significance of Ananda Coomaraswamy" wisdomlib-org

    https://www.wisdomlib.org/concept/ananda-coomaraswamy

- Osho (Bhagwan Shree Rajneesh):

  - Online Resource: osho.com. "Osho Official Website." Osho.com.

    https://www.osho.com/

- Brahma Kumaris:

  - Online Resource: brahmakumaris.org. "Brahma Kumaris Official Website." BrahmaKumaris.org.

    https://www.brahmakumaris.org/

III. Scientific & Academic References (Neuroscience, Biology, Anthropology, etc.)

- On Mindfulness & Meditation (Neuroscience):

  - Kabat-Zinn, Jon. Wherever You Go, There You Are: Mindfulness Meditation in Everyday Life. Hyperion, 1994.

  - Lazar, Sara W., et al. "Meditation experience is associated with increased cortical thickness." Neuroreport, vol. 16, no. 17, 2005, pp. 1893-1897.

  - Online Resource: mindful.org. "Mindful.org: Healthy Mind, Healthy Life." Mindful.org.

    https://www.mindful.org/

  - Example of specific article: Davidson, Richard J. "Mindfulness and the Brain." Greater Good Magazine. Greater Good Science Center at UC Berkeley.

    https://greatergood.berkeley.edu/article/item/mindfulness_and_the_brain

- On Interconnectedness/Ecology:

  - Capra, Fritjof. The Tao of Physics: An Exploration of the Parallels Between Modern Physics and Eastern Mysticism. Shambhala, 1975.

  - Online Resource: deep-ecology.net. "The Deep Ecology Movement." Deep Ecology Network.

    https://www.deep-ecology.net/

- On Rituals & Community (Anthropology/Neuroscience):

  - Sosis, Richard, and Eric Alcorta. "Signaling, Solidarity, and the Sacred: The Evolution of Religious Ritual." Evolutionary

Anthropology: Issues, News, and Reviews, vol. 12, no. 6, 2003, pp. 264-274.

○ Online Resource: scientificamerican.com. "The Neuroscience of Group Bonding." Scientific American.

https://www.scientificamerican.com/article/the-neuroscience-of-group-bonding/

- On Identity in Digital Age:

○ Turkle, Sherry. Alone Together: Why We Expect More from Technology and Less from Each Other. Basic Books, 2011.

○ Online Resource: pewresearch.org. "Pew Research Center: Internet & Technology." Pew Research Center

https://www.pewresearch.org/internet/

- General Science/Neuroscience:

○ The Self-Aware Universe: How Consciousness Creates the Material World. Jeremy P. Tarcher/Putnam, 1993

○ When the Body Says No: Understanding the Stress-Disease Connection. John Wiley & Sons, 2003

○ Kak, Subhash C. The Wishing Tree: Presence and Promise of India. DK Printworld, 2015

○ Roy, Raja Ram Mohan. Vedic Physics: Scientific Origin of Hinduism. Createspace Independent Publishing Platform, 1999

○ Majumdar, Mrittunjoy Guha. From Shiva to Schrödinger: Unravelling Cosmic Secrets with Trika Shaivism and Quantum Insights

○ Online Resource: research.miu.edu. "Modern Science and Vedic Science Journal". modern-science-and-vedic-science-journal

https://research.miu.edu/modern-science-and-vedic-science-journal/

- Online Resource: vedicheritage.gov.in. "Science – Vedas – India's Science Base". Vedicheritage-gov

  https:// vedicheritage.gov.in.gov.in/science/

- Online Resource: vedicscience "Indian Foundation for Vedic Science" vedicscience

  http://vedicscience.website2.me/

- Online Resource: eternalreligion.org "scientific knowledge sanatan dharma" eternalreligion.org

  https://eternalreligion.org/wp-content/uploads/2019/08/scientific-knowledge-sanatan-dharma-3.pdf

- Atul, Tripathi. Quantum Physics & Vedic Philosophy: Where science meets spirituality, 2025

- Online Resource: bharatabharati.in "Quantum Physics & Vedic Philosophy" quantum-physics-vedic-philosophy-where-science-meets-spirituality

  https://bharatabharati.in/2025/03/11/quantum-physics-vedic-philosophy-where-science-meets-spirituality-atul-tripathi/